JOHN
GRISHAM

Other titles in the Greenhaven Press Literary Companion to Contemporary Authors series:

Tom Clancy
Michael Crichton
Stephen King
J.K. Rowling

The Greenhaven Press
LITERARY COMPANION
to Contemporary Authors

JOHN GRISHAM

Nancy Best, *Book Editor*

Daniel Leone, *President*
Bonnie Szumski, *Publisher*
Scott Barbour, *Managing Editor*

**GREENHAVEN
PRESS®**

THOMSON
™
GALE

San Diego • Detroit • New York • San Francisco • Cleveland
New Haven, Conn. • Waterville, Maine • London • Munich

LIBRARY OF CONGRESS CATALOGING-IN-PUBLICATION DATA

Readings on John Grisham / Nancy Best, book editor.
   p. cm. — (The Greenhaven Press literary companion to contemporary authors)
Includes bibliographical references and index.
ISBN 0-7377-1665-7 (pbk. : alk. paper) — ISBN 0-7377-1664-9 (lib. : alk. paper)
   1. Grisham, John. 2. Legal stories, American—History and criticism. 3. Novelists, American—20th century—Biography. I. Title: John Grisham. II. Best, Nancy. III. Series.
PS3557.R5355Z84 2003
813'.54—dc21   2002045483

Printed in the United States of America

Contents

Chapter 1: An Introduction to John Grisham and His Work

   John Grisham had practiced law for three years when
   he heard a twelve-year-old girl testify against the man
   who raped her. Realizing that if it had been his daughter who was raped he would kill the perpetrator, Grisham began his first novel, *A Time to Kill.* Grisham has
   been trying cases in print ever since.

   Grisham attributes his success to the fact that his novels are fast-paced, easy-to-read legal thrillers that are
   relatively clean. Grisham believes that fame is temporary, which is why he strives to live a normal life despite his success.

   Grisham writes simply plotted, easy-to-follow fiction.
   His style is flowing and his books have happy endings.
   These and other factors contribute to his commercial
   success.

   John Grisham has turned from rejection slips to

megasales. He has three rules for developing a story: a beginning that grips readers and hooks them for a ride, a middle that sustains them with narrative tension, and an ending that sets them on the edges of their seats.

Grisham's success as a writer is due to more than just the content of his stories. He has also developed a process for writing his best-sellers. He starts with ideas from real-life cases. He works with a team of researchers and legal experts for background material, then outlines an entire novel before he begins writing.

Chapter 2: John Grisham and the Genre of the Legal Thriller

In Grisham's stories, the legal system is presented as an obstacle to America's righting itself, and so his heroes often subvert the rules to win their battles.

Though the emphasis of the American legal system is conservative adherence to the law, Grisham's stories feature heroes who bend or even subvert the law in order to achieve justice.

Grisham's stories often feature graphic scenes of violence, yet Grisham has publically condemned the violent portrayals in movie director Oliver Stone's work.

Chapter 3: Themes and Issues in Grisham's Novels

In Grisham's novel *The Firm*, the young protagonist

Mitch McDeere must use all his intelligence to outwit not only his own corrupt law firm but also the FBI. In a time of increasing distrust of basic institutions, Grisham's heroes are idealistic individuals who are willing to battle the corruption of those institutions to survive. This is the root of their popular appeal.

his usual populist formula of modern-day David and Goliath tales. Instead of fighting institutionalized corruption, this protagonist must deal with the moral dilemma of finding $3 million in cash.

FOREWORD

Contemporary authors who earn millions of dollars writing best-sellers often face criticism that their work cannot be taken seriously as literature. For example, throughout most of his career, horror writer Stephen King has been dismissed by literary critics as a "hack" who writes grisly tales that appeal to the popular taste of the masses. Similarly, the extremely popular Harry Potter books by J.K. Rowling have been criticized as a clever marketing phenomenon that lack the imagination and depth of classic works of literature. Whether these accusations are accurate, however, remains debatable. As romance novelist Jayne Ann Krentz has pointed out:

> Popular fiction has been around forever but rarely has it been viewed as important in and of itself. Rarely have we acknowledged that it has a crucial place in culture. . . . The truth is, popular fiction—mysteries, science fiction, sword and sorcery, fantasy, glitz, romance, historical saga, horror, techno-thrillers, legal thrillers, forensic medical thrillers, serial killer thrillers, westerns, etc.—popular fiction is its own thing. It stands on its own. It draws its power from the ancient heroic traditions of storytelling—not modern angst. It is important, even if it is entertaining.

Although its importance often goes unrecognized, popular fiction has the power to reach millions of readers and to thus influence culture and society. The medium has the potential to shape culture because of the large and far-flung audience that is drawn to read these works. As a result of their large readership, contemporary authors have a unique venue in which to reflect and explore the social and political issues that they find important. Far from being mere escapist fiction, their works often address topics that challenge readers to consider their perspectives on current and universal themes. For example, Michael Crichton's novel *Jurassic Park*, while an entertaining if disturbing story about what could happen if dinosaurs roamed the planet today, also explores the potential negative consequences of scientific advances and the ethical issues of DNA experimentation. Similarly, in his 1994 novel *Disclosure*, Crichton tells the story of a man who suffers predatory sexual harassment by his female supervisor. By reversing the expected genders of the victim and aggressor, Crichton added fuel to the debate over sexual politics in the workplace.

Some works of fiction are compelling and popular because they address specific concerns that are prevalent in a culture at a given time. For example, John Grisham has written numerous novels about the theme of corruption in America's oldest legal and business institutions. In books such as *The Firm* and *The Pelican Brief*, courageous though sometimes naive individuals must confront established, authoritarian systems at great personal danger in order to bring the truth to light. Written at a time when government and corporate scandals dominated the headlines, his novels reflect a faith in the power of the individual to achieve justice.

In an era when 98 percent of American households have a television and annual video sales outnumber book sales, it is impossible to ignore the fact that popular fiction also inspires people to read. The Harry Potter stories have been enormously popular with both adults and children, setting records on the *New York Times* best-seller lists. Stephen King's books, which have never gone out of print, frequently occupy four to five shelves in bookstores and libraries. Although literary critics may find fault with some works of popular fiction, record numbers of people are finding value in reading these contemporary authors whose stories hold meaning for them and which shape popular culture.

Greenhaven Press's Literary Companion to Contemporary Authors series is designed to provide an introduction to the works of modern authors. Each volume profiles a different author. A biographical essay sets the stage by tracing the author's life and career. Next, each anthology in the series contains a varied selection of essays that express diverse views on the author under discussion. A concise introduction that presents the contributing writers' main themes and insights accompanies each selection. Essays, profiles, and reviews offer in-depth biographical information, analysis of the author's predominant themes, and literary analysis of the author's trademark books. In addition, primary sources such as interviews and the author's own essays and writings are included wherever possible. A comprehensive index and an annotated table of contents help readers quickly locate material of interest. In order to facilitate further research, each title includes a bibliography of the author's works and books about the author's writing and life. These features make Greenhaven Press's Literary Companion to Contemporary Authors series ideal for readers interested in literary analysis on the world's modern authors and works.

INTRODUCTION

John Grisham is one of the most popular writers of contemporary fiction in the world, yet he began his working life, not as a writer, but as an attorney. In fact, the basis of Grisham's fiction, which virtually defines the genre of the legal thriller, lies in his early career as a lawyer. Within a few years of opening his practice, he had grown weary of the profession. There in his office, he began writing his first novel, a story inspired by a case he had witnessed at the local county courthouse. Over the years since then, in one novel after another, written at the breakneck pace of one per year, Grisham has explored many of the issues he dealt with in his own practice. Issues that often had no satisfactory resolution in real life could be shaped and molded into stories with richly satisfying conclusions, stories that sold by the millions, making Grisham one of the wealthiest writers in the world.

Early on, Grisham discovered the type of story that worked for him, one that makes use of the archetypal characters of David and Goliath. Grisham's heroes are usually bright, yet naive, lawyers just out of law school. Typically they encounter long-standing American institutions that have become riddled with corruption, such as insurance companies, tobacco companies, local police departments, federal agencies like the FBI and CIA, or established law firms representing huge conglomerates. These young lawyers get involved in cases that lead them beyond the normal scope of legal practice into life and death issues, and that put them and other characters in the novel in harm's way.

In a Grisham story, the identity of the villain is seldom a

mystery, yet they are usually people the average American is brought up to trust rather than challenge. They are political leaders, heads of corporations, or respected members of the legal establishment—people in authority. While in many thrillers, the novel's suspense hangs on who has committed a crime, in Grisham's stories, the suspense is centered in how the already identified villain, who is immensely powerful, will be brought down.

The stories follow a pattern that is appealing to Americans' sensibilities: The individual challenges authority to defeat overwhelming odds. In Grisham's version of the David vs. Goliath myth, the idealistic young attorney outwits the villain, bringing institutionalized evil to light by breaking the rules created by those very institutions. The hero must bend the rules or go against established values in order to bring truth to light. In the end the individual prevails.

Although there are some critics who laud Grisham's work, comparing him to Charles Dickens and John Steinbeck (both of whom also dealt with social corruption in their works), others contend he is writing formulaic tales whose outcomes are too easy to predict. Grisham shrugs off such criticism, saying that he is convinced that were the critics to like him, the book-buying public would not.

Though Grisham does not aspire to write literary fiction, he has often felt the pressure from those who judge his work on literary terms. This was especially true when he took up residence in Oxford, Mississippi, the home of the Nobel Prize–winning author, William Faulkner. Grisham wrote an essay in the acclaimed literary magazine, the *Oxford American*, entitled "The Faulkner Thing," in which he lamented the challenge of being constantly queried about and compared to the great writer. A reporter had cornered him at a bookstore and in response to her insinuating comments about the difficulties he must face in such a comparison, Grisham wrote,

> I'm not a Southern writer. . . . I'm a commercial writer
> who lives in the South. I try to write commercial fic-

tion of a high quality—no attempt at literature here—
just good books that people enjoy reading. The libraries are already filled with great literature. There's
no room for me.

Judged on his own terms, however, Grisham is phenome-
nally successful. In a society where corporate scandals
abound and where there is growing mistrust of the institutional authority, Grisham has himself become an institution:
a writer who knows exactly the type of story that is certain
to sell.

JOHN GRISHAM: A BIOGRAPHY

By most measures, John Grisham is one of the most success-ful living writers in America. He has published fourteen books—a book every year since his first novel, *A Time to Kill,* and all have become best-sellers. His book sales now surpass horror writer Stephen King's and romance author Danielle Steele's. In 1996 alone, Grisham's books brought him over $40 million in royalties, and sales have increased each year since then, making him one of the wealthiest writers in the world.

Grisham's success is not limited to his work. He has been happily married to his childhood sweetheart, Renee, for more than twenty years. He and his wife, along with their two chil-dren, live in a palatial home in Virginia on one hundred acres of land, complete with a handyman and a live-in house-keeper. The Grishams have another home on nearly sixty acres of land in Oxford, Mississippi. Grisham also owns his own jet airplane. As if all this were not enough, Grisham is perhaps the only writer in America to be listed in *People* mag-azine's annual list of the "50 Most Beautiful People."

GRISHAM'S EARLY YEARS

John Grisham's prodigious success has surprised many people, not least of all himself, since nothing in his early years sug-gested he would become either rich or famous. John Grisham was born in 1955 in Jonesboro, Arkansas, the second of five children of John Grisham Sr. and Wanda Grisham. The elder Grisham was a construction worker who moved to wherever he could find a job. As a consequence, for the first twelve years of John Grisham's life, the family moved often, from one southern town to another. Construction work was hardly lucrative, and when they grew big enough, the Grisham children picked cotton at their grandparents' farm to earn their own spending money. Despite the financial difficulties, the Grishams were a happy and stable family. Grisham fondly recalls much storytelling around the dinner table.

Early on, John Grisham's parents instilled in him the value of reading, encouraging him and the other children to read for entertainment, rather than watch television. Each time the family moved to a new town, Grisham's mother took the children to the library, where, after receiving library cards, the children would check out as many books as the rules allowed.

Grisham's mother was a powerful influence on his life beyond encouraging him to read. Grisham describes his mother as a very pious woman who, each time the family moved to a new town, would immediately join the local Southern Baptist church. Wanda Grisham saw to it that her children attended church too. John and his siblings, scrubbed and dressed in their best clothes, would attend services every Sunday morning. The children did not seem to mind these Sunday mornings and indeed took church seriously. John, for example, at age eight committed himself to following the principles of Christianity in his life.

A MEDIOCRE STUDENT

Eventually, the Grishams' nomadic lifestyle changed. John Grisham Sr.'s work took the family to Southaven, Mississippi, a suburb of Memphis, Tennessee, in 1967. John attended both junior high and high school there, graduating from Southaven High School in 1973.

Despite his mother's encouraging him to be a reader, however, John was at best a mediocre student. He had little interest in most of his classes and was a "C" student, though one of his English teachers recalls that young Grisham enjoyed reading. What John Grisham loved most was playing baseball, and he dreamed of one day achieving a place in the Baseball Hall of Fame. Yet although Grisham played on his high school's team, he clearly lacked the talent needed to make a career in baseball. Without a clear sense of direction, he enrolled at Northwest Junior College in Senatobia, Mississippi, where he could at least play baseball during his freshman year.

What emerged during the next years was a growing lack of purpose in Grisham's life. He transferred from one school to another, at first with the hope that he might continue playing baseball. He tried out for the baseball team at Delta State in Cleveland, Mississippi, but the competition to make the team at the four-year school was harder than it had been at Northwest Junior College. Grisham did not make the team that first semester, and he doubted his ability to succeed in the future. He found it especially difficult to hit a fast ball or a curve ball, and he knew the game well enough to know that good pitchers would be brutal when they spotted any weakness of that sort.

At least partially because of his failure to make the team, Grisham and his roommates left Delta State after only one semester. The friends enrolled in Mississippi State University in Starkville, a halfhearted move during which they made backup plans for yet another transfer, to Appalachian State University in Boone, North Carolina, if things did not work out.

GRISHAM'S TURNAROUND

At first it looked as though things would not work out for Grisham at Mississippi State. He was still not a good student and he recalls that he was not interested in learning. But that first semester at MSU, Grisham enrolled in an economics class that changed his attitude toward school. He witnessed a class session in which the students in the class engaged in a lively dialogue with the professor. These students were prepared, articulate, and unafraid of challenging authority. This experience deeply impressed Grisham. He decided that was what he wanted for himself—the confidence and intellectual engagement he witnessed in that classroom.

Grisham's grades were not good, but he set out to salvage them with hard work. He immediately switched his major to economics, although shortly thereafter he decided that accounting suited him even more. His goal was admittedly purely monetary: to attend law school and become a wealthy tax attorney.

Grisham's attitude toward school had improved dramatically, but he had a backup plan should he not get accepted to a law school he liked. His father had opened his own business in Southaven, and Grisham thought that, at the very least, with an accounting degree he could help his father. Grisham's grades and abilities, however, had improved dramatically, and despite a "D" in an English composition course, he graduated with a B.S. in accounting from Mississippi State in 1977; the next year he was accepted into law school at the University of Mississippi in Oxford.

GRISHAM'S LAW CAREER

At the University of Mississippi, Grisham quickly became disenchanted with tax law. The rules seemed to change every day, and he had no interest in spending all his time keeping up with all the new rules. But he discovered he was good in mock court, where students take turns playing various roles in simulated trials. Once, taking the role of the defendant in such a trial, Grisham was so convincing—unshaved and wearing a worn T-shirt—that the students serving as his attorneys had trouble defending him.

Grisham liked the dramatic aspect of this type of law. His propensity for quickly grasping the stories and situations of those in difficult circumstances and his ability to play to an audience would be helpful in a courtroom. Grisham, therefore, switched his specialty to criminal law. After he graduated from law school in 1981, Grisham returned to Southaven, where he opened his own practice.

With him was his childhood sweetheart, Renee, whom he had married during his last year of law school. Grisham practiced law for almost a decade, specializing in criminal and personal injury law. He won his first case, defending a man who had fatally shot his lover six times after she had first shot him. Grisham often served as a court-appointed attorney for defendants who could not afford to pay for legal representation, so he did not make a lot of money. Still, on what he earned, he and Renee lived comfortably in a two-bedroom brick house.

GRISHAM'S TERM IN THE MISSISSIPPI STATE LEGISLATURE

Grisham's practice gradually grew, but despite this success, he was bored with the law. He wanted to make positive changes in the world. He had become interested in politics during law school, so in 1983 he ran for the Mississippi state legislature on the Democratic ticket. In his campaign, Grisham advocated improving public education. Grisham spoke to National Public Radio's Terry Gross, recalling his decision: "I was embarrassed because at the time," said Grisham, "Mississippi was the only state with no public kindergarten system, and I wanted to be elected to the legislature and to work hard for public education in Mississippi." In 1983 the voters of Mississippi's Seventh District elected Grisham to represent them in the Mississippi House of Representatives.

His election meant some personal sacrifice for Grisham. The state legislature met in Jackson, and Grisham lived several hundred miles away in Southaven. While the legislature was in session he stayed in Jackson, sharing living quarters with two other lawmakers. This was a busy time for Grisham. Not only did he keep up his own practice while in the legislature, but now he had another avocation, writing fiction. His roommates remember him, locked away in his room, writing when he was not at work making laws.

Grisham served two terms as a state representative. In his second term he held positions on important House committees and was vice chairman of the Appointment and Elections Committee. Yet he was often frustrated with politics and the difficulties of accomplishing anything he considered worthwhile. Sometimes bored by the frequent periods of inactivity of the legislature, he once introduced a resolution commending Herbert Khaury (who in actuality was Tiny Tim, a singer popular for his parodies of American sentimentality with songs like "Tiptoe Through the Tulips").

GRISHAM'S FIRST NOVEL

The fiction Grisham was working on was a novel. During his years in Oxford, Grisham had become an avid reader of bestsellers and had even started to write a novel then, although he had abandoned that work entirely. This new effort, however, Grisham was determined to complete. It would prove to be his first published novel, *A Time to Kill.*

The idea for the story came from a trial Grisham personally observed at the county courthouse. During those early days of Grisham's legal career, if he had little to do, he would spend time at the county courthouse, especially if good lawyers were in town trying challenging cases. At the time a white man had been accused of raping a twelve-year-old black girl. The crime was so heinous and the case so widely publicized that everyone knew when the trial was scheduled to take place. Grisham went to the county courthouse to watch the proceedings. Although the court was closed to the public during the victim's testimony, Grisham was allowed to stay because the judge knew him. The child's testimony was so wrenching that several members of the jury, the prosecutor, and even the judge wept. Grisham's own daughter had not yet been born, but he knew that had this happened to his own child, he would have killed the defendant if he had the chance.

The court was cleared during a break in the girl's testimony, and Grisham, in his haste to leave the courtroom, left his briefcase behind. He walked through the back entrance of the courthouse, up the back stairs, and through a side door into the courtroom to retrieve it. There, he found himself alone in the courtroom with the defendant and a single deputy. At that moment it dawned on Grisham how easy it would be for someone to take revenge for the child's rape, and at that moment the idea for Grisham's novel was born. He went home and began writing. In *A Time to Kill*, the father kills the men who assaulted his daughter; much of the plot concerns the resulting trial of the father for murder.

Grisham worked on the novel for three years, finding time to write early in the morning, on weekends, or whenever he could. Meanwhile, he was busy establishing his own practice and continued to serve on the state legislature. Grisham and Renee also started their own family. They had their first child, Ty, in 1984 and their second child, Shea, in 1986. Grisham would be at his office by five-thirty. He would turn on all the lights to reinforce the impression among people who passed by that he was a very hardworking lawyer. When he had spare moments at work, he jotted down ideas on legal pads.

In 1987, after finishing the novel, Grisham sent it out to nearly thirty publishers and agents. It was turned down by all of them. Finally, in 1989, two years after he finished it, an editor named Bill Thompson read the manuscript and offered Grisham a fifteen-thousand-dollar advance for the novel. Fewer than five thousand copies of the book were printed. Grisham personally bought one thousand copies and sold them out of the back of his car, begging local bookstores to sponsor readings and selling copies to friends and acquaintances. (Those copies of the first edition are now worth over four thousand dollars each.)

DISCOURAGING SALES

Grisham was disappointed with the sales of *A Time to Kill.* He had aspirations for commercial, not literary, success. Seeking to make his next book more saleable, Grisham carefully developed the story line for *The Firm*, a story about a young tax attorney who unwittingly takes a job for a law firm that launders money for organized crime.

Grisham was skeptical about his own premise for the novel, wondering if such a hero would arouse the reader's empathy. But his wife and hardest critic, Renee, liked his idea. He finished the novel, and in the fall of 1989 sent it to his agent in New York, Jay Garon. Garon showed the manuscript to a number of publishers, but no one was interested in publishing it. Somehow, though, a bootleg copy of the manuscript mysteriously landed on the desk of a Hollywood producer who copied it and sent it out to all the major studios.

Unbeknownst to Grisham, this started a bidding war. One Sunday while Grisham was in church, Renee slipped in and told him he had received a phone call: Paramount had offered six hundred thousand dollars for the film rights to *The Firm*. With Hollywood so clearly interested in the novel, Garon soon had a publisher for *The Firm*. Grisham's second novel was an instant hit: 550,000 hardbook copies and 7 million paperback copies were sold.

GRISHAM BUILDS HIS REPUTATION

Grisham was ready now to give up both his law practice and his seat in the Mississippi state legislature to become a full-time writer. After Grisham closed his practice in Southaven, he and Renee built a large Victorian house on fifty-seven acres of land near Oxford. Grisham felt that there he could devote himself to his writing while Renee finished her studies at the University of Mississippi.

Despite his financial success, Grisham kept up the same grueling pace in his writing that he had maintained as a lawyer and legislator. The day after he completed a novel, he got up at 5:30 A.M. and began a new novel. He read five newspapers each day, looking for potential material; he also had teams of lawyers and researchers working for him since, by his own admission, he had never enjoyed research.

Grisham now turned out one novel a year, and always his strategy was the same. He began by outlining an entire novel before he wrote anything else. These outlines were usually over forty pages long with one or two paragraphs on each chapter, though he did not feel compelled to follow the outline as the novel progressed. His tactic was simple: to hook the reader on page one and keep the reader turning pages until the end of the story. He did this by getting the story's protagonist into trouble and then figuring out a way to save him or her. The point was to keep the plot moving, even if that meant not developing scenes or detailed descriptions fully.

Grisham's third book, *The Pelican Brief*, was also an enormous success, selling 1.4 million hardback copies and 5.1 million paperback copies. The story pitted a young female law student against a corrupt and wealthy businessman who was willing to do anything, including assassinating two Supreme Court justices, in order to promote his own business interests. Darby Shaw, the female hero, follows the usual pattern for Grisham's protagonists: A bright young individual with little experience and little power is pitted against institutional heavyweights, in this case the FBI and corrupt business interests. When the movie based on the novel came out, Grisham was invited to the White House for a private screening. There, he shared a bucket of popcorn with President Bill Clinton and First Lady Hillary Rodham Clinton.

Since the publication of *The Pelican Brief* in 1992, Grisham has published eleven novels, or a book a year (except in 2001, when he published two books, *A Painted House* and *Skipping Christmas*). The novels include *The Client*, 1993; *The Chamber*, 1994; *The Runaway Jury*, 1995; *The Rainmaker*, 1996; *The Partner*, 1997; *The Street Lawyer*, 1998; *The Testament*, 1999; *The Brethren*, 2000; *A Painted House*, 2001; *Skipping Christmas*, 2001; and *The Summons*, 2002.

PLANS FOR THE FUTURE

As Grisham gained popularity as a writer of legal thrillers, he and his wife found they had little privacy in Oxford. Tourists came in profusion to see Faulkner's home, and many of them also made a stop at Grisham's farm. Once he and Renee even woke up one morning to find a couple exchanging marriage vows in their pasture. To regain some privacy, in 1996 the Grishams moved to a two-hundred-year-old Colonial mansion on one hundred acres of land near Charlottesville, Virginia.

Grisham frequently expresses the opinion that success in the world of commercial fiction is short-lived. He compares the arc of his career to that of an athlete's career, saying that it could be over any day. He has expressed a willingness to branch out into other areas. In 2001 Grisham published two novels, both of which diverged from the genre of legal thriller. *The Painted House* was initially published serially in the *Oxford American*. It is a semiautobiographical work in which Grisham draws on the family tales he recalls from his childhood. *Skipping Christmas*, published the same year, is a comic novel about a middle-aged couple who makes plans to spend Christmas away from home. However, much to the relief of fans of his legal fiction, he published another thriller, *The Summons*, in 2002.

Despite his continued popularity as a writer, what Grisham most likes to do is spend time coaching baseball. When he learned that there were no Little League fields in Charlottesville, he donated the money to build a complex of playing fields. Most weekends he can be found there, marking off the field or helping to keep score.

To this day Grisham considers his success as a writer fleeting: "I firmly believe all this is temporary," he said in an interview for the *Saturday Evening Post*. "It will be over one of these days—five years from now, ten years from now. The books will stop selling for whatever reason." But then, writing best-selling legal thrillers has never been the most important thing in Grisham's life. He has repeatedly ranked his faith, his relationships, and his love of baseball as more important than selling books. Still he keeps on writing bestsellers, a new one every year. These best-selling stories feature Grisham's ever-popular hero, the ordinary man or woman, defeating institutionalized corruption.

CHAPTER 1

An Introduction to John Grisham and His Work

READINGS ON
JOHN GRISHAM

Grisham's Novels Reflect His Personal Experience

Geoff Williams

In this profile of John Grisham, Geoff Williams gives an account of how a real-life criminal case was the basis for Grisham's first published novel. Grisham had practiced law for three years when he walked into a courtroom and heard a twelve-year-old girl testify against the man who had raped her. Realizing that if it had been his daughter who was raped he would kill the perpetrator, Grisham began his first novel, *A Time to Kill.* "He's been trying cases in print ever since," Williams observes. Williams goes on to touch on other aspects of Grisham's past and present life and shows how real events and people find their way into his books. Geoff Williams is a regular contributor to Compuserve's online publication, *Wow!*

The 12-year-old girl had been raped. Now she was living through the crime again, only this time in front of a judge, a jury, her attacker, and an audience of interested onlookers. One of those onlookers was a 29-year-old lawyer with a little time to kill.

With the rapist just a pebble's toss away, the girl recounted her nightmare. John Grisham shifted uneasily in his seat, watching, listening, and simmering with rage. He mentally discarded everything he had learned in law school about due process and the ponderous workings of the legal system. He thought instead about what he would do had it been his daughter who was raped and who was giving testimony. And what he imagined was standing up in the courtroom with a powerful

Geoff Williams, "A Brutal Crime, a Passion for Justice," *Biography*, vol. 1, January 1997, p. 68. Copyright © 1997 by *Biography* magazine. Reproduced by permission.

gun in his hand and blowing away his child's molester.

It could have been a scene straight out of a book or movie, and it would be. Grisham avenged the girl in his first novel, *A Time to Kill,* and he's been trying cases in print ever since. In fact, over 60 million copies of those cases are on bookshelves everywhere. Or maybe you've never heard of *The Firm, The Pelican Brief, The Client, The Chamber, The Rainmaker,* or *The Runaway Jury?*

Grisham's Early Years

John Grisham, Jr. was born in Jonesboro, Arkansas, on February 8, 1955, the only fanfare coming from parents John and Wanda and older sister Beth (Kenny, Mark, and Wendy came into the story later). As the family grew, the Grishams traveled: John, Sr. joined a construction crew which necessitated various moves around the South until the family finally halted in Southaven, Mississippi, a suburb of Memphis, Tennessee. Southaven was the cornerstone setting in the life of John Grisham, then 12 years old. It was here that he met future wife Renee Jones, thrived on his high school football and baseball teams, and submerged himself in the Mississippi mindset that figures so prominently in his novels.

There was little evidence then that one of Southaven's own would become a literary legend, acknowledges Laverne Davis, who became close with the senior Grishams shortly after their arrival. Davis remembers the parents as strict— "Mrs. Grisham kept a firm hand on them"—and the children as well behaved. But John, Jr. had a silly side, says Davis, who often saw him at their Southern Baptist church and later when she was a secretary at his high school. Davis recalls Grisham telling tall tales about his family and of fictional wild adventures, and she says his imaginative muscles flexed throughout high school, but she "never did dream he would turn out to be the writer he is."

Evelyn Sims didn't guess either, though her student fared well in the 11th-grade literature class. Sims recalls Grisham as a popular student who loved reading almost as much as swinging a bat or passing a football. Few clues revealed that Grisham would become a writer, but Sims does remember more than a passing interest in politics and law.

GRISHAM'S COLLEGE YEARS

He wanted to be a baseball player. After graduating in 1973, Grisham played at Northwest Mississippi Junior College and after a year transferred to Delta State University, hoping to make their team and eventually turn professional. But during try-outs, Grisham twice dove for cover as the ball torpedoed across the plate, effectively ending his baseball career.

Transferring to Mississippi State University, his field of dreams turned to accounting. If nothing else, he could help his father, who had recently started his own heavy-equipment dealership. Thoughts of being a tax lawyer also began to develop.

As did a flirtation with writing. During his senior year in 1977, Grisham started scrawling down a novel set in rural Mississippi. He eventually trashed it and concentrated on classes and an upcoming career.

"I was rather smug and confident, perhaps even a bit arrogant because I, at the age of 22, had already figured out my life," Grisham concluded 15 years later, as a best-selling novelist addressing his alma mater. "I had it all planned and was certain things would fall neatly into place. I had earned my degree in accounting. I had been accepted to law school where I planned to study tax law and one day soon make lots of money representing rich people who didn't want to pay taxes."

Mitch McDeere in *The Firm* would achieve these goals, but not Grisham, who switched his focus at law school from finances to felons. (Years later, Dora Herring, Grisham's cost accounting teacher at MSU, would ask, "John, if you could do it over, would you take a major other than accounting?" Not at all, Grisham replied, admitting that the logic he learned was useful in plotting complicated novels. "It might be that he was being nice to me," concedes Herring. "He would have said that, even if he didn't really mean that. It's part of a Southern gentleman veneer.") During law school, the Southern gentleman made another unsuccessful stab at finishing a novel, its plot involving international terrorists on a college campus. In 1981, his senior year, Grisham married childhood sweetheart, Renee, in a small wedding.

His degree came next, and with it the law license. What never came were offers of employment. Not one firm offered him a job.

Grisham hired himself. He opened a practice with a lawyer in Southaven and soon had a successful business. In 1983, Grisham's son, John Tyler, was born, and the lawyer decided to use his judicial skills statewide: as a legislator in the Mississippi House of Representatives.

"He was real organized," says Scott Ross, elected the same year as Grisham. During the three months per year the politicians were required to work in the capital, Ross and another freshman, Bobby Moak, roomed with Grisham during the week. "Every day he'd have a legal sheet of things that still had to be done, and he'd try to conduct the law practice over the telephone," recalls Ross.

For most of 1984, the 29-year-old Democrat tackled legislative duties and numerous cases at his firm, by now a solo practice, but late in the year something happened, that defining moment which finally inspired the dormant novelist within him to write a story. Grisham strolled into a courtroom and heard the stunning testimony of the 12-year-old girl who had been raped. Sickened, Grisham knew that if he had a daughter (Shea was born two years later) and she was attacked, he'd murder the rapist. It was the birth of *A Time to Kill.*

GRISHAM WRITES HIS FIRST NOVEL

And the death of free time, not that Grisham ever had any. The author later reminisced to *Writer's Digest:* "I wrote with the flu, on vacation, with no sleep, in courthouses when I could sneak off to a quiet room for 30 minutes, in the state capitol building in Jackson. I carried a legal pad with me in my briefcase and wrote on it."

"He was always in his room, locked up," confirms Bobby Moak, the third roommate. Moak and Ross would hear Grisham's bedroom door shut around 9 P.M. "Of course, we were downstairs having a beer, going, 'What in the world is he up to?' And we would hear him shuffling around at 4:30 the next morning, and sometimes we wouldn't see him for a couple of days."

During those days of early drafts, only Renee was privy to reading Grisham's work. Ross notes that he and Moak never saw a word of the book until its completion.

Moak and Ross admired Grisham's family values, which he practiced before it was a political buzzword. Observes Ross: "In the legislature, if you are so inclined, it's quite easy to play around. If he had wanted to, he could have had the opportunity, and not even once did he consider it. He was entirely faithful to his wife and family the whole time. He told me, 'No, when I made the decision to get married, that was it.'"

He was rejected by 15 agents and 26 publishers before his first book was finally released in 1989. Grisham received $15,000, and 5000 copies were initially printed. Bill Thompson, the editor who bought *A Time to Kill*, and who discovered [best-selling horror writer] Stephen King, clearly recognized untapped talent, but booksellers were underwhelmed, and it fell to Grisham, Moak, and Ross to sell the volume to stores themselves.

Grisham's Second Novel Brings Financial Success

Several booksellers exhibited interest, but most didn't, and by the time the 5000 copies had been sold or given away, Grisham had finished *The Firm*. It was 1990. Grisham was presented a $600,000 check from Doubleday, the publisher.

Thanks to *The Firm*, Grisham closed his own legal firm to write full time, and he resigned from the legislature, giving his seat to family friend Greg Davis, son of Laverne. "When I first got down there," Greg recalls, "they kept talking about the big shoes I would have to fill by taking his seat."

True enough. This was a man who—aside from being a member on a slew of committees—had been badgered to run for the U.S. Senate. But former fellow representative Ayres Haxton believes Grisham was only too happy to part with the political world. "I think John was disillusioned with the way state government works—as are a lot of idealistic people—'cause it's, uh, it's been compared to making sausage, and I think that's a good comparison. You really don't want to see what's in sausage. When you see it, it's somewhat disillusioning, and I think he had enough of it."

He's also had enough with fame. After moving to a sprawling farm in Oxford, Mississippi, Elvis fans gawking at nearby Graceland too often made the house part of their tour, and so the Grisham family purchased a second home in the relative seclusion of Charlottesville, Virginia. Nevertheless, Grisham tries to maintain a normal life. Ever the baseball fan, he still coaches his son Tyler's Little League team.

"I think you could safely say that his teams have a lot better players than they have coaches," snickers Ross.

Don't worry. He'll pay for those comments in a future novel. John Grisham delights in casting his friends in his books. Most buddies—like Ronnie Musgrove, a law student classmate and now the lieutenant governor of Mississippi—have found their names attached to minor but moral characters. However, Moak and Ross usually end up as two-bit thugs. For instance, Ross admits, "I think I'm a juvenile delinquent in *The Client,* and I'm on death row in *The Chamber.*"

Each summer brings a new Grisham yarn, and more often than not a box-office bonanza based on one of those books. While Grisham is usually content to let Hollywood perform radical surgery on his stories (he claims never to have visited that town), he does involve himself in elements of the filmmaking—even to the point of delaying production for a year on last summer's [1996] film, *A Time to Kill*, because he didn't feel the lead had been correctly cast. Only when Grisham gave his approval to Matthew McConaughey was it time for *Time* to film. And for all the high-brow critics decrying Grisham's contribution to pop culture, they can't deny the author's assistance to the literary journal *The Oxford American,* the South's answer to *The New Yorker.* Shortly after *The Pelican Brief,* Grisham wrote "The Faulkner Thing" for the premiere issue of *The Oxford American.* Several issues later, Grisham asked the editor how the magazine was doing. "It was teetering," Marc Smirnoff confessed, so Grisham volunteered his financial help and his name (he's listed as publisher). He continues to be a major investor. "Simply put, without John, there would be no *Oxford American,*" says Smirnoff, who currently moonlights as the editor of Grisham's novels before they go to the publisher.

And in an age of stadium-size bookstores, Grisham hasn't forgotten the smaller ones that believed in him from the beginning. His annual book tour consists of five establishments, three of them in Mississippi and one in Memphis. Grisham hardly needs the exposure, but his visits aid proprietors like Mary Gay Shipley, owner of That Bookstore in Blytheville, Arkansas. She accepted early copies of *A Time to Kill* and—a rarity back then—actually requested more.

Shipley remembers Grisham's first book-signing at her store, which coincided with the day *The Firm* hit the bestseller list. Grisham arrived early for the signing, and when the store opened, he was sitting on the curb, next to his pickup truck, looking nervous. Today, Grisham arrives in Blytheville in a Lear jet, those original copies of *A Time to Kill* are worth several thousand dollars, and the writer is recognized wherever he goes, whether dining in town or traveling across the country. How will the attorney-turned-author deal with his increasing popularity? What's next for the writer known around the world? Even John Grisham probably doesn't know. He hasn't written that chapter yet.

Grisham's Novels Reflect His Christian Faith

Will Norton Jr.

Will Norton Jr. interviews John Grisham about his unexpected success as a writer of legal thrillers. Grisham tells Norton that he never planned to be a writer; he was inspired to write his first novel after witnessing a real-life trial. Grisham attributes his own success to the fact that his novels are fast-paced, easy-to-read legal thrillers that are relatively clean. Grisham also expresses his belief that fame is temporary and says this is why he strives to live a normal life despite his success. Will Norton Jr. is dean of the College of Journalism at the University of Nebraska-Lincoln and a former professor at the University of Mississippi, where Grisham attended law school.

If you drive about 50 miles south from Memphis on Interstate 55 along the edge of the fertile Mississippi delta, you could turn east on Highway 6 through the hill country of north Mississippi made famous in the novels of William Faulkner, a Nobel laureate whose home has become an attraction for hundreds of literary scholars each year.

You would be driving toward Oxford, the small town where leading figures of the New York publishing world descended to bury Faulkner in the summer of 1962.

Oxford has nurtured some of America's great writers. One of the most commercially successful of these is John Grisham. Grisham was a virtually unknown small-town lawyer until hitting the bestseller lists with five successive novels. *Newsweek* called Grisham a "commercial supernova." Sales of

Will Norton Jr., "Why John Grisham Teaches Sunday School," *Christianity Today*, vol. 38, October 3, 1994, p. 14. Copyright © 1994 by Christianity Today, Inc. Reproduced by permission.

his novels *A Time to Kill, The Firm, The Pelican Brief, The Client,* and *The Chamber* now exceed 40 million.

From Oxford, Grisham has written a novel a year until he moved with his family to Charlottesville, Virginia [in 1993]. The mass media have written a great deal about Grisham the writer, but it is not common knowledge that Grisham committed his life to Christ when he was eight years old. He remains dedicated to living according to biblical principles as he copes with the fame and wealth thrust on him since 1990.

Will Norton Jr.: Some analyses of your novels say that they're about greed. Are they?

John Grisham: They're about lawyers. I don't know if the two go hand in hand. I was a lawyer for ten years, so I write about what I know. I take normal people, almost all of whom happen to be attorneys, and they get in really stressful situations and try to get out of them. It's not a magic formula.

How did you learn to write?

It wasn't something I'd always wanted to do. I never dreamed of being a writer when I was a kid or even when I was a student. When I was a third-year law student at Ole Miss in 1980 or '81, I tried to write the first chapter of a novel and didn't get very far. I more or less forgot about it. Then I saw something in a courtroom a few years later that inspired me to create what I thought was a powerful courtroom drama. One day I said, I'm going to see if I can put this on paper. I sat down and wrote the first page. When I finished the first page, I wrote the second. Before I knew it, a chapter was finished, and it became kind of a hobby. But I never made the decision, "I'm going to be a writer." It was very gradual and unplanned.

Why do your books sell so well?

I've read a lot of analyses: The books are very enjoyable. They have a certain flow and level of suspense so they can be read quickly. People get caught up in them. One thing that helped is that the books are relatively clean, and when *The Firm* was published, a lot of people bought the book and realized they could give it to an older teenage son or daughter or to their parents. So the books were passed around. I hope it says something about our culture that you can be successful without succumbing to all the gratuitous sex and language that is so prevalent today. Another reason is that the American reading public and movie and television audiences have had an insatiable appetite for stories about lawyers, courtroom drama, law firms, and shenanigans.

You're now worth millions of dollars. Is it daunting to make so much money so quickly?

It's unsettling. It's happened in two years, but we were comfortable before this happened. I had been practicing law for ten years and working very hard. So we were not going without anything. But you struggle when all this money is dropped on your lap; you ask, "Why has it happened to me? What am I supposed to do with it?" We've always had the attitude that the fame is temporary. It's very much like the career of an athlete. There are some good years and bad years, but one of these days it will be over, and we've always said that we hoped we would look back and say it was fun while it lasted, we kept our feet on the ground, we didn't change, and it's time to go on to something else.

You told college students at North Oxford Baptist Church that there was a particular experience in your life that prepared you for having this kind of attitude.

One of my best friends in college died when he was 25, just a few years after we had finished Mississippi State University. I was in law school, and he called me one day and wanted to get together. So we had lunch, and he told me that he had terminal cancer. I couldn't believe it. I asked him, "What do you do when you realize that you are about to die?" He said, "It's real simple. You get things right with God, and you spend as much time with those you love as you can. Then you settle up with everybody else." That left an impression on me.

A number of gifted writers have come from the South. In

what ways has living in the South formed your writing?

I was born in Jonesboro, Arkansas, and we moved all over the Deep South. My father worked for a construction company, and he was transferred every year or two, depending on where the work was. We lived in Arkansas, Mississippi, and Louisiana. I had to adjust to new situations, new schools, and new people. We did not have a lot of money, and that was not important to us. The first thing my family did when we moved was join the local Southern Baptist church. The second was go to the public library and get library cards. My mother did not believe in television. I grew up reading books, and I'm sure that inspired me to be a writer. My father's family is a family of storytellers, and there were long dinners and lots of stories. As children, we absorbed them.

What do you remember of your conversion?

I was eight years old. We lived in Arkansas at the time. Back then, my father often worked seven days a week. My mother had us bathed and scrubbed and in church every Sunday. She's a devout Christian. I came under conviction when I was in the third grade, and I talked with my mother. I told her, "I don't understand this, but I need to talk to you." We talked, and she led me to Jesus. The following Sunday I made a public confirmation of my faith. In one sense, it was not terribly eventful for an eight-year-old, but it was the most important event in my life. It did not readily change me, but it was very real nonetheless.

You were involved in mission trips with the First Baptist Church of Oxford. And you and your wife have taught Sunday school. What lies behind that?

During my childhood in the Baptist church we would hear wonderful stories and see slides from all over the world. I always wanted to take part in mission work and never really was able to do it for the ten years I was busy practicing law. Finally, I was able to go to Brazil last year with about 40 other people from this county. We went to a remote area of the country and built a church in four days. We took two doctors, a dentist, and a couple of nurses with us: two or three medical teams. As for Sunday school, we're not teaching this year, but we have. I taught various classes where we lived before, and my wife, Renee, taught the three- and four-year-old children.

Do you ever ask, "Why me, God?"

Yes. I used to ask all the time. I'm getting used to the success, but the questioning still hits occasionally. I go for long walks in the woods a lot, and I ask myself if I'm handling it the way it ought to be handled. I don't know why it happened to me. God has a purpose for it. We are able to contribute an awful lot of money to his work, and maybe that's why. But I firmly believe it will be over one of these days—five years from now, ten years from now. The books will stop selling for whatever reason. All this is temporary.

The Factors Contributing to John Grisham's Commercial Success

Sean French

Sean French, columnist for the *New Statesman & Society*, analyzes John Grisham's position on the best-seller list. Grisham's writing habits and publishing records are compared to writers of popular fiction, such as Stephen King and Scott Turow, as well as the great Russian novelist Fyodor Dostoyevsky. Like Stephen King, Grisham turns out one best-seller after another with apparently little effort. Like Turow, he has used his law background to find material for his best-sellers. Unlike Dostoyevsky, Grisham writes simply plotted and easy-to-follow fiction. After writing his first book, *A Time to Kill*, in a southern literary style, Grisham searched for ideas for thrillers that would work in a legal setting. His idealistic heroes confront corrupt, yet established villains. Having little inner conflict, Grisham's young idealists are successful at every turn despite their inexperience. His great success with these stories often mystifies his critics. Besides his flowing style, Grisham's success is attributed to the American public's desire for a happy ending.

Some critics find thriller-writer John Grisham's success bizarre. They underestimate the American public's desire for a nice happy ending.

When I was away for a week's holiday I took two books: *The Brothers Karamazov* by Fyodor Dostoyevsky, first published in 1880, and *The Rainmaker* by John Grisham, first

Sean French, *New Statesman & Society*, vol. 8, June 9, 1995, p. 35. Copyright © 1995 by *New Statesman & Society*. Reproduced by permission.

published last week [June 1995]. I have so far reached page 180 out of 776 pages of *Karamazov* and page 434 out of 434 pages of *The Rainmaker*.

THE WORLD'S MOST POPULAR AUTHOR

Let's take John Grisham first. "I do not begrudge him a comfortable living from what are, to my mind, mildly diverting second-division legal thrillers," said Marcel Berlins, reviewing the book in the [*New York*] *Times*. Yeah, yeah, Marcel, pull the other one. "But," Berlins continued sourly, "Grisham's grip on the bestseller lists is beyond understanding." That's putting it a bit strongly, but can there be any writer who could read the author's biography on the dust jacket of *The Rainmaker* without a little stab of pain. Here it is in its entirety: "John Grisham is the most popular author in the world. His five previous books (*A Time to Kill, The Firm, The Pelican Brief, The Client* and *The Chamber*), have all been number one bestsellers worldwide and have sold over 60 million copies in the English language." Not very literate, but it has a certain ring to it, don't you think?

HOW HE DOES IT

There's something equally dismaying about Grisham's account, in the introduction to his first novel, of how he wrote that novel, "much like a hobby, with a somewhat disciplined effort to write at least a page a day." I've got a special cavity in my brain where I store depressing accounts of how very successful writers have written their books. Scott Turow wrote *Presumed Innocent,* one of the half-dozen best thrillers of the past ten years, on the train to and from his law firm each day. Why couldn't he just sit and stare into space the way other people do on trains?

And there's the likeable, but also deeply gloom-inspiring, afterword by Stephen King to his collection of novellas, *Different Seasons*. He explains where they come from: "Each of these longish stories was written immediately after completing a novel—it's as if I've always finished the big job with just enough gas left in the tank to blow off one good-sized novella. *The Body*, the oldest story here, was written directly after *Salem's Lot; Apt Pupil* was written in a two-week period following the completion of *The Shining; Rita Hayworth and Shawshank Redemption* was written after finishing *The Dead Zone*; and *The Breathing Method*, the most recently written of these stories, immediately following *Firestarter*."

The Writers Who Never Suffered Writer's Block

Why should this harmless paragraph be so upsetting? Well, those days where you get to about four o'clock and you realise that children are coming home from school now and you haven't written anything yet, they're depressing enough already, but now you can think at the same time of Stephen King, who, after he has completed a big novel, writes a little novel as a way of slowing down. Then those four little novels were put together to make another very pig (I meant to type "big," but I'll trust to serendipity and let it stand) book of over 550 pages. And furthermore, it's not just that each of the four big novels—*Salem's Lot, The Shining, The Dead Zone, Firestarter*—were made into major Hollywood films (the middle two of which are remarkable), two of the novellas were made into good films as well, *The Shawshank Redemption* and *Stand By Me* (from *The Body*).

King will probably now publish a fat volume of short stories he wrote while winding down from his novellas and then of poems he wrote while winding down from his short stories and haikus he wrote while winding down from his poems. And they'll all be filmed as well. Has he never heard of writer's block?

Movie Themes Influence Grisham's Work

You can see Marcel Berlins' point about Grisham. In his neo-Gothic field, Stephen King is some sort of genius and *Presumed Innocent* is the sort of book Saul Bellow might produce if he tried to write a George V. Higgins thriller. But there doesn't seem much to John Grisham, especially if, like me, you've apparently seen the same films he has. I would guess that after his first novel, which is written in a consciously southern literary style, Grisham searched around for thriller ideas he could transfer to a legal setting. *The Firm* is about an idealistic man who joins a successful Memphis law firm and discovers everybody is criminal. It resembles most strikingly the film and Ira Levin book, *The Stepford Wives*, in which the men in a small town share the guilty secret that they have replaced their wives with androids. *The Pelican Brief* is about an apparently minor discovery which forces a young legal student to go on the run, just as Robert Redford does in *Three Days of the Condor*.

Grisham's books really do flow past you very pleasantly, partly because there are no difficult conflicts in them. He recalls the dictum that what the American public wants are tragedies with happy endings. There is a revealing episode in *The Firm* in which the hero, Mitch, is tempted into being unfaithful to his wife. He is photographed and blackmailed by a thug at the law firm. You wait for the conflict this causes between Mitch and his wife, but nothing happens. The episode gets forgotten about. Grisham writes weirdly reassuring thrillers in which the hero never gets into any danger.

WHY THE READER LIKES GRISHAM

You know those haunted-house pictures where somebody says: "We'll be all right if we stay together," and then somebody replies: "All right, I'll just go and check the cellar door is locked"—and they go down to the cellar and after lots of alarms get stabbed to death; and then a woman says she'll just go to get her cat and she gets killed and so on. Well if John Grisham wrote a haunted-house novel, they all would stay together and there would be nothing to worry about and at the end you would feel nice and relaxed, rather than as if your internal organs had been run through a wringer.

This is even more true of *The Rainmaker*, which is the story of a rather leek-less, totally inexperienced young lawyer who becomes involved in a major court action on his own against a large, corrupt insurance company and a brilliant legal team. You expect that there will be awful tension as the wicked opposition play dirty tricks on him, spring surprises on him, manipulate the system, twist the law, blackmail witnesses. Nothing of the kind. He outwits them at every stage with brilliant resourcefulness, the judge is completely on his side and people emerge from the woodwork to provide him with crucial documents that blow the opponents' case apart. It's nothing but a series of triumphs.

Like shooting fish in a barrel, you may say, but so what? Every year I go fishing in this lake where my relatives live in Sweden and every year I fail to catch anything at all and return to the shore sour and resentful. If somebody could provide a barrel with some fish in it, I would be quite happy to shoot a few of them. It may be easy, but it would at least guarantee a certain satisfaction.

And *The Brothers Karamazov*? Well, there are those Russian names for a start. Alexei Fyodorovich Karamazov, for example, is also referred to as Alyosha, Alyoshka, Alyoshenka, Alyoshechka, Alexeichik, Lyosha and Lyoshenka. It sometimes seems as if there are enough brothers to make up Moscow Dynamo on their own. And if Grisham is like shooting fish in a barrel, Dostoyevsky is like looking for them on the open sea.

What Success Has Taught John Grisham

Michelle Bearden

In this 1993 article in the trade journal *Publishers Weekly*, Michelle Bearden relates how Grisham managed to bring his experiences as a small-town lawyer to bear as an author of legal thrillers. In speaking with Bearden, Grisham says his goal for his first book, *A Time to Kill*, was "simply to finish it." Grisham talks about the commercial success of his second novel, *The Firm*, the movie rights to which he sold before it was even published. Grisham relates to Bearden his response to criticism of his third novel, *The Pelican Brief*, and muses on his relationship with Hollywood and on the way he is compared to another writer of legal thrillers, Scott Turow. Florida-based writer Michelle Bearden is a frequent contributor to *Publishers Weekly*.

This is what happens when you cross that line between relative obscurity and international recognition: actor Wilford Brimley, who's playing a pivotal role in a forthcoming movie based on your bestseller, takes stock of your 70-acre spread and decides a quarter horse is just what you need. So he makes a selection from his personal stables at his Utah ranch and ships it all the way to Oxford, Miss., where you live.

Makes no difference that you don't know the first thing about equestrian matters. It's the thought that counts, and the knowledge that once you've arrived, life is full of grand gestures and surprises.

"At first I wasn't sure if the bridle was supposed to go on me or the horse," admits John Grisham, recipient of Brimley's

Michelle Bearden, "An Interview with John Grisham," *Publishers Weekly*, vol. 240, February 22, 1993, pp. 70–71. Copyright © 1993 by *Publishers Weekly*. Reproduced by permission.

gift and author of the phenomenal bestsellers *The Firm, The Pelican Brief* and *A Time to Kill.*

"The guy who delivered him had to give me a few lessons on the spot. But now we're going to buy three more so the whole family can ride together."

What Grisham lacks in horse sense, however, he certainly makes up for in the ability to write a suspenseful story. If early reviews are any indication, his newest effort, *The Client,* out from Doubleday next month (Fiction Forecasts, Feb. 1 [1993]), promises to follow in the triumphant footsteps of his three previous books, which topped 1992 bestseller lists in cloth and paperback.

At 38, a relatively young age to have it all, John Grisham appears remarkably untouched by the whirlwind success that has made him one of America's hottest writers. When *PW* [*Publishers Weekly*] meets him at his Victorian home in Oxford on a slate-gray January morning, he's your basic ordinary guy, marked with a stubble of beard and dressed in a blue denim workshirt that matches his eyes, fretting about some mundane concerns. His wife is weathering the flu, party plans for his daughter's seventh birthday are under way and Bo, the lumbering chocolate Labrador, has abandoned his assigned security role and is smothering the visitor with sloppy dog kisses instead. Oh, and Grisham also is trying to figure if he can juggle plans to attend his distant cousin's inauguration.

GRISHAM'S AFFILIATION WITH BILL CLINTON

"Bill Clinton and I may be distantly related," he says matter-of-factly, in a measured Southern drawl. Grisham also shares political affiliation with his relative, having served seven years as a Democratic member of the Mississippi state legislature. Politics, he learned, was much like his first career, law: at times exciting and challenging, but for the most part, downright frustrating.

He could say the same for writing, at least in the early days. In 1984, just three years out of Ole Miss law school and running a one-man criminal defense practice in South-haven, Miss., Grisham got the itch to write a novel. Specifically, a courtroom drama, based on a gut-wrenching case he had observed involving a young girl who had to testify against the man who had brutally raped her. Watching the girl suffer, Grisham could not even imagine the nightmare she and her family had endured. He became obsessed with the idea of retribution and yearned to shoot the rapist. "For one brief moment, I wanted to be her father. I wanted justice. There was a story there."

GRISHAM JUGGLES WORK AND WRITING

That tale of paternal revenge became *A Time to Kill,* written in the predawn hours over three years as he juggled a taxing 60- to 80-hour work week plus three months a year in the state House of Representatives. A son, Ty, now nine, then daughter, Shea, joined Grisham and Renée, the girl next door whom he married after law school. Looking back, he admits that much of the 1980s is now a blur, and that he was just too busy to worry about whether the book would ever get published.

Recalls Grisham: "Because I have this problem of starting projects and not completing them, my goal for this book was simply to finish it. Then I started thinking that it would be nice to have a novel sitting on my desk, something I could point to and say, 'Yeah, I wrote that.' But it didn't consume me. I had way too much going on to make it a top priority. If it happened, it happened."

In the beginning, it almost felt as if it wouldn't happen. First, there was the task of finding an agent. In early 1987, Grisham sent off dozens of manuscripts and got a few responses, but nothing concrete. Finally in April, Jay Garon of New York called and told Grisham he wanted to represent him. Why did he accept? "He was the only one who said he'd mail a contract immediately," Grisham says.

Garon says there was no doubt he had discovered a natural-born storyteller with immense talent. "I smelled a winner right off the bat," he tells *PW*. "That was the easy part. The hard part was trying to convince a market that is leery about new writers to give him a chance." Garon peddled *A Time to Kill* for about a year, amassing a slew of rejections before finally making a deal with Bill Thompson of the now-defunct Wynwood Press for $15,000—the same Bill Thompson who had bought *Carrie* from a newcomer named Stephen King years earlier (and who now runs a packaging company called The Literary Group). *A Time to Kill* was published in June 1989, in a 5,000-copy printing.

"I bought 1,000, and another 1,000 were sitting in a warehouse, so you know not many were out there," Grisham acknowledges. But now he was halfway into his second novel, *The Firm*, a story he was only lukewarm about but one that "made Renée go berserk." Because she is his best editor and most vocal critic—"She makes those people in New York look like *children*"—Grisham stayed with the project. He completed it in September, and Jay started the peddling process again.

THE FIRM TAKES A DIFFERENT TWIST

Only this time, the story took a different twist. Grisham had no idea that a bootleg copy of his still-unpublished book had landed in the hands of West Coast filmmakers, so he was caught completely off guard that first Sunday in January 1990 when Renée tracked him down at church. Garon had called from New York, she relayed breathlessly, and John needed to call him immediately. Apparently Hollywood wanted to buy *The Firm*.

Grisham went to bed that night a rich man. Paramount had plunked down $600,000 for the movie rights to a manuscript that no publisher had yet seen fit to buy. The following day, news of the deal lit up phone lines on both coasts. Within two weeks, Grisham had a contract with Doubleday—one of the many houses that had passed on *A Time to*

Kill two years earlier. "I still have the rejection letter," he says, with a hint of a smile.

The year 1990 evolved into one of Grisham's most memorable. First there were the deals surrounding *The Firm*; then Renée's father, a contractor, began building the house of their dreams on a former horse farm in Oxford; and finally, Grisham decided to quit the legislature and close his law practice so he could write full-time. He did all this without the guarantee that *The Firm*, scheduled for March 1991 publication, would fulfill its promise.

THE FIRM: 47 WEEKS ON THE BESTSELLER LIST

Not to worry. *The Firm* enjoyed a whopping 47 weeks on the *New York Times* bestseller list after it was released; in 1992, it topped *PW*'s list of longest-running paperback bestsellers with 48 weeks. His next book, *The Pelican Brief* (Doubleday), became 1992's longest-running hardcover bestseller, staying on the *PW* list for 42 weeks. And after Doubleday acquired the paperback rights and republished *A Time to Kill*—the novel that remains dearest to Grisham's heart—it claimed the No. 2 spot last year on *PW*'s longest-running paperback bestseller list at 27 weeks. To date, combined sales worldwide for the three books have topped an astronomical 17 million copies.

If that isn't enough good fortune, three of Grisham's books will hit the screen within two years. *The Firm*, directed by Sidney Pollack and starring Tom Cruise, Brimley and Gene Hackman, is slated for release in July; filming on *The Pelican Brief*, directed by Alan Pakula, will begin in May. Director Joel Schumacher wants cameras rolling in June for *The Client*.

Grisham hasn't written the screenplays for any of his books, nor does he wish to. Hollywood, he says, isn't his scene. "I sell the film rights for a lot of money, I kiss it goodbye and I move on. No one puts a gun to my head. If the movies bomb, you won't hear me moaning and mouthing off."

Grisham still considers himself a lawyer, but he is ecstatic that he doesn't have to practice anymore. In fact, he says, "Most lawyers I know would rather be doing something else." It appears at least half of them are budding novelists, as evidenced by the glut of attorneys turned writers these days. About this, Grisham is not surprised: "Law provides lots of juicy material, lurid situations, scummy characters. The plots are practically handed to you." In his humble opinion, only three are masters of the genre, which means handling the legal terminology without bogging down the reader: himself, Scott Turow (*Presumed Innocent, The Burden of Proof* and the forthcoming *Pleading Guilty*) and Steve Martini (*Compelling Evidence*).

"Turow's *Presumed Innocent* was the first, and it's a classic," says Grisham of the legal-suspense wave. "People make a big deal over comparing us. We're both lawyers and we're both writers, but that's where the similarities end. I think people would like to see us duke it out, but that's not going to happen. There's plenty of room for both of us. And in the end, the good books sell and the bad ones don't."

Criticism of *The Pelican Brief* Hits Grisham Hard

Not one to take success for granted, Grisham is nervously anticipating reaction to *The Client*, the first book in a three-book deal he has with Doubleday. Even though *The Pelican Brief* sold millions, some critics blasted it. That hit Grisham hard, because he had placed so much importance on repeating his earlier acclaim. "It's the American way," he shrugs. "As a rookie, people were really pulling for me with *The Firm*, but the second time around, those same people were secretly wishing I would fail so they could rip me to shreds."

This time, Grisham has vowed not to get upset by critics, and to focus on reader reaction instead. In writing *The Client*, he concentrated mainly on character development—an effort that shouldn't go unnoticed, says Doubleday's David Gernert, Grisham's editor since *The Firm*. "This was a very brave, very smart move for John. It is different from his other books, yet he doesn't lose the twists and elements that make him such a compelling writer. He has that ability to combine suspense with subtle and effective humor, and create characters that are just human, not extraordinary. In the case of John's books, it's really true: you can't put them down."

GRISHAM'S RULES FOR SUCCESS

Grisham, who always begins writing his next book at 5 A.M. the morning after he sends a completed manuscript off to New York, says he follows three rules in developing his stories: A beginning that grips readers and hooks them for a ride, a middle that sustains them with narrative tension, and an ending that sets them on the edges of their seats. The characters tend to be ordinary people sucked into a conspiracy that puts their lives in danger. "And always, there's something dark, shadowy and sinister lurking in the background."

If Grisham has any regrets about his meteoric rise, it is that success has come so fast he hasn't had the chance to savor it. He has slowed his pace considerably from last year, giving fewer interviews and making fewer appearances so he can spend more time with his family. In April, he heads to a remote location in Brazil with fellow members of the First Baptist Church in Oxford on a mission to help erect buildings for the villagers. It will be a delight, he says, to be around people who have no interest in books or movies.

Story ideas continue to race in his head, which is good news for Grisham fans. He compares a writer's career to that of an athlete, noting that at some point, it's time to retire the uniform. "There's nothing sadder than a sports figure who continues to play past his prime," Grisham says.

But if and when the words run out, John Grisham will probably do what he does best—change careers. In 10 years, he has already done what most never accomplish in a lifetime, having mastered three professions—lawyer, politician, bestselling author—with enviable ease. What next? Without hesitation, he answers, "A Little League baseball coach. Now that's where you can have some *real* fun."

John Grisham's Strategy for Writing Best-Sellers

Mel Gussow

New York Times reviewer Mel Gussow outlines John Grisham's strategy for writing successful legal thrillers. Having once been a practicing attorney, Grisham has no shortage of ideas. He begins his day by reading five newspapers, "I'm continually looking for stories," he says. Each story begins with a reality. He hires a team of lawyers to guard against copyright infringement and he also hires research assistants to do background work. With each novel he does a chapter-by-chapter outline of the entire story. His aim is to write a book that is plot-driven and that can be quickly read. His books have an air of authenticity because of his legal expertise, which according to Grisham, leads his readers to think of them as "fact, not fiction." Grisham says of his critics, "I've succeeded in spite of them. They butcher my books, and they keep selling." He considers turning to more literary works when he has exhausted the legal fiction genre.

John Grisham writes a double-edged brand of escapist fiction. A Grisham is a page-turning legal thriller in which the leading character often takes the money and runs. In the latest, *The Partner*, a lawyer steals $90 million from his firm and its wealthiest client, fakes his own death and flees to Brazil.

"For lawyers, the main dream of escape is get out of the profession," Mr. Grisham said in a recent interview. "They dream about a big settlement, a home run, so that they can use the money to do something else."

This is basically what Mr. Grisham did. As a struggling young lawyer, he turned to writing fiction, which is what one of his law professors at the University of Mississippi had suggested in the first place. Through a series of novels published over the last decade, he has become, at 42, one of the most successful authors of popular fiction.

How Grisham Escaped the Law

With 2.8 million copies in print, *The Partner* opened in the No. 1 position on the *New York Times* best-seller list on March 16 and remains there. At the same time, last year's [1996] Grisham novel, *The Runaway Jury*, a quick-moving investigation of jury manipulation during a lawsuit against tobacco firms, is at the top of the paperback fiction list.

Mr. Grisham himself has taken the money and run, all the way to Hollywood, which routinely turns his novels into movies. Three Grisham movies are in various stages of development and production. One of his earlier films, *The Pelican Brief*, had its premiere at the White House. Mr. Grisham was born in Arkansas, and he said, "President Clinton is my 16th cousin. One of his grandfathers was named Grisham."

Exuding confidence and well-being, the author was in Manhattan on a whirlwind day trip from his home in Charlottesville, Va. In the morning he signed his new novel at the Borders bookstore at the World Trade Center, while Barnes & Noble halved the price of the book in order to meet the competition.

The number of signed copies was limited to 200, but Mr. Grisham took time to chat with each reader: suburban mothers with babies as well as lawyers and law students. Watching with silent approval were his agent and a covey of representatives of his publisher, including Jack Hoeft, the president and C.E.O. of the Bantam Doubleday Dell Publishing Group.

For Mr. Grisham, fiction is not only the most remunerative of livelihoods, but also a chance, he said, to "get back at people, chew 'em up: big law firms and insurance companies, arrogant judges and lawyers." Clearly, this is also what appeals to his readers.

"The profession is terribly overcrowded," he said, "not only in New York City, where you have 50,000 lawyers, but also in small towns. It's tough to make a good living. There is so much needless litigation, because lawyers are looking for business."

He admitted that he had a natural cynicism about his former occupation, although, paradoxically, the response to his books from lawyers has been largely positive. Most lawyers he knows, he said, are "honest and hard-working and don't make a lot of money, but people don't want to read about them." The protagonist of his new novel is intended to be morally ambiguous: "I wanted to show that with money you can really manipulate the system. You can buy your way out of trouble."

THE GRISHAM FORMULA

In most Grishams, the reader follows the financial trail, which often leads to the Cayman Islands. "The narrative has to be almost relentless," he said. "You can't slow down to explore a good meal or talk about the scenery," or spend time on romance.

Not quite so. Although sex does not figure prominently in his books, there is always food on the table: crab claws and gumbo in *The Partner*. That fact, Mr. Grisham said, once provoked his wife, Renee, to comment wryly in an interview that her husband knew more about food than sex. At all costs, his aim is to write a book that is plot-driven and can be read in two or three days, almost without stopping.

When Mr. Grisham was practicing law, he disliked preparing briefs, and he feels the same about doing research. He hires assistants for leg (and legal) work. Because of his expertise, the books have an air of authority, which leads his readers to think of them "as fact, not fiction," he said.

Each story begins with reality. *The Partner* is based on several fugitive lawyers, including one from Mississippi who faked his death and then went to his own funeral. He was angry because not all his friends were there. Mr. Grisham thought of the Brazilian location for the novel when he visited that country with a church group that was building a chapel.

GRISHAM OUTLINES HIS PROCESS

Before he begins a book, he does a chapter-by-chapter outline, but he is not necessarily sure of the outcome. With *The Partner*, he had two alternate endings. With *The Firm*, there were a half-dozen possibilities: "People have said they messed up the movie because they changed the ending. Well, I wasn't sure how to end it either."

Generally a book takes him six months to write, leaving him ample time for Little League activities with his two children. He built his own ball park near his home and acts as commissioner of the local league.

His first book, *A Time to Kill*, was submitted to a score of agents and publishers before it was accepted. It became a bestseller and a movie only after he made his reputation with his other books. Nevertheless, in 1991, before *The Firm* was published, he closed his law office and became a full-time writer.

He wrote a screenplay, which was rejected. Now, of course, anything he touches is a hot property. Rewritten, the rejected screenplay is being filmed by Robert Altman under the title *The Gingerbread Man.*

WHERE GRISHAM GETS HIS IDEAS

In search of ideas, Mr. Grisham starts his day by reading five newspapers. "I'm continually looking for stories," he said. "Almost every event becomes grist for a novel." People also send him ideas, and partly to guard against copyright infringement, he has a team of lawyers on retainer.

Although he searches for the unusual, he keeps up with high-profile cases. "Right now, we have a trial of the century every year," he said. "I tried to ignore O.J., which is impossible."

On one point Mr. Grisham is adamant: He is firmly opposed to cameras in the courtroom. While mining the news, he also tries to think of "unknown theories of liability and crimes that have yet to be committed; you have to have a hyperactive imagination."

On request, he offered a sampling of potential Grishams.

High-powered ambulance chasers: "An airplane goes down, and disaster lawyers are on the scene before the paramedics. One lawyer got caught because he had someone dressed as a priest go into a crash site and console the families. The outright solicitation of disaster victims is just sickening."

Jailhouse lawyers: "At the State Penitentiary at Parchman, Miss., there's a law library where writ writers hold court. These are the most important people in prison, because every guy there obviously has serious legal problems. They sit down with inmates and negotiate a fee—cigarettes, television, sex—and then they crank out a writ."

GRISHAM'S PLANS FOR THE FUTURE

Only when Mr. Grisham has exhausted the profession, or it has exhausted him, does he plan to turn to other pursuits, which may include writing something he would consider "more literary," the kind of books he likes to read. (His favorite author is John Steinbeck.) As of now, there is no end of Grishams in sight, and critics are not about to slow him down: "I've succeeded in spite of them. They butcher my books, and they keep selling."

"Everything in popular culture is cyclical," he said. "I keep waiting for people to get tired of legal thrillers and courtroom dramas, but there is no sign of a decrease in interest." As for subject matter, "You can always find lawyers who have done worse things than I can ever dream up."

CHAPTER 2

John Grisham and the Genre of the Legal Thriller

How Grisham Influences the Public's View of American Justice

Terry K. Diggs

Terry K. Diggs analyzes the legal thriller and how it defines the popular vision of the American justice system in this comparison of authors John Grisham and Scott Turow. Grisham's version of the legal thriller features the quintessential American hero—hard-working and idealistic—trying to prevail against a corrupt system. In Grisham's stories, the legal system is presented as an obstacle to America's righting itself, and so his heroes often subvert the rules to win their battles. Turow's heroes are not young idealists, but long-time practitioners of the law, caught up in their own compromises. In Turow's fiction, there are no pure clients, no pure lawyers. Everyone is corrupt. The law does not exist to solve the most basic problems of the human condition, it exists as a measure of our willingness to involve ourselves in the business of life, and in this, Turow's heroes find their redemption. Both writers greatly influence the American public's vision of the legal system. Terry K. Diggs, a San Francisco attorney and writer, teaches a course on law and popular culture at the University of California's Hastings College of the Law.

John Grisham and Scott Turow lay down the law for millions of Americans. Just what is it they're trying to tell us?

Over seven days in October [1996], millions of Americans who balk at their own lawyers' hourly rates will cheerfully pay top dollar to enter the fictional worlds of John Grisham and

Terry K. Diggs, "Through a Glass Darkly," *ABA Journal*, vol. 85, October 1998, p. 74. Copyright © 1998 by Terry K. Diggs. Reprinted by permission.

Scott Turow. *The Chamber*, the film version of Grisham's 1994 best seller, opens on Oct. 11. Turow's newest novel, *The Laws of Our Fathers*, debuts the following week.

The new offerings promise equal helpings of evidence and ethos, portraying radically dissimilar visions of the American justice system.

Grisham and Turow are not shouting in the wilderness, of course, but producing images for mass consumption. Their plaintiffs go platinum. Their bailiffs and bondsmen are boffo. Their powerful pictures of justice are what your clients, your family and your jury pools know best of due process.

Both are masters of traditional American narrative genres and shrewd adapters of the storytelling patterns that have always stirred our ardor and stymied our analysis. Given their power to mesmerize, shouldn't someone be watching these guys a bit more closely? Shouldn't we care who is laying down the law?

TRACING THE INFLUENCES ON GRISHAM'S STORIES

Grisham's stories take their tone from the tales of the Great Depression. *The Firm*'s Mitch McDeere, the ambitious Harvard grad who winds up among treacherous tax lawyers, recalls the character James Cagney played in a half-dozen Warner vehicles—films where a poor boy makes good by falling in with the wrong crowd and must extricate himself before the credits roll.

Grisham's 1993 best seller, *The Client*, replicates the same post-Crash plotline that made [movie] stars of Jackie Cooper and Dickie Moore—the winsome urchins who took adult partners on the lam. In *The Client*, Grisham's canny kid flees the government and the goons, abetted by a wisecracking family practitioner, Reggie Love.

In *The Chamber* (1994), a young lawyer, Adam Hall, copes with the execution of his grandfather, a former terrorist for the Ku Klux Klan. Grisham's plot seems borrowed from the trial of Byron De La Beckwith, assassin of Medgar Evers, but it also recalls Hollywood's traditional treatment of death row. Like the condemned in Woody Van Dyke's *Manhattan Melodrama* (1934) and Michael Curtiz's *Angels with Dirty Faces* (1938), Grisham's sympathetic bad guy must take the long walk in the last reel—a political reminder that capital punishment's personal cost is outweighed by public policy.

GRISHAM'S SIMILARITIES TO FRANK CAPRA

But it is [Hollywood director] Frank Capra, the would-be moralist who defined prewar America in a legion of films— *It Happened One Night* (1934), *Mr. Deeds Goes to Town* (1936), *Mr. Smith Goes to Washington* (1939), *Meet John Doe* (1941), etc.—whose philosophical bent Grisham apparently shares. Capra's spirit pervades Grisham's heartland heroes who conquer the Beltway [Washington, D.C.'s power center] (*The Pelican Brief,* 1992), the couples who wage war on corrupt corporations (*The Runaway Jury,* 1996), and the average Joes fighting extraordinary avarice (*The Rainmaker,* 1995).

Grisham's protagonists, like Capra's, emerge from outside the metropolis, only to face the ridicule of the power elite.

They bring to the fracas values we recognize as quintessentially American: wholesomeness, resilience and common sense. They prevail by turning the skills in legal procedure, technology and finance that mark them as go-getters toward thwarting a corrupt system.

Grisham places them at the top of their law school classes, but in doing so he manages—as Capra so often did—to render intellectualism suspect: When scholarship imperils his heroes—with good grades in *The Firm* (1991) and brilliant research in *The Pelican Brief*—it is plain old resourcefulness that delivers them from danger.

Grisham's lawyer-heroes are outside the conventional bar. They are mavericks who practice on the fringe, scraping by like Jake Brigance, the small-town, solo practitioner of *A Time to Kill* (1989). Or they are law students who abort their studies (*The Pelican Brief*'s Darby Shaw, who stumbles on a plot to overthrow the government).

Or they are recent graduates whose attempts to practice draw fire from the "old boys"—the fate of *The Rainmaker*'s Rudy Baylor, whose travails in finding work make melodrama of the experiences of recent law graduates.

Grisham's outsiders evoke Capra's appealing outlaws, displaying a sensibility that ultimately disdains the law and despises its practitioners. Capra saw lawyers as doubly damnable, the architects of the New Deal and the engineers of the crisis that necessitated it.

Yet Capra's city shysters—the hired guns of *Mr. Deeds* or *You Can't Take It with You* (1938)—are no more sinister than *The Pelican Brief*'s White & Blazevich, Washington superlawyers who deal with bad precedent by murdering judges, or *The Runaway Jury*'s Whitney & Cable & White, silkstocking strategists who augment their practice with burglary and bribery.

Grisham may imperil his protagonists with the odd international terrorist, neo-Nazi contract killer or PAC [Political Action Committee] mastermind, but the threat to justice is inevitably orchestrated at the partnership level of the mandarin firm.

In Grisham's world, as in Capra's, law is too much with us, with every operation of law creating yet another obstacle to America's righting itself. Thus, Grisham's heroes—'90s models of Deeds and Smith—do justice by engaging the law in its lair and vanquishing it.

GRISHAM'S SUBVERSION OF THE LEGAL SYSTEM

Yet Grisham's schemes too often reveal something that is genuinely frightening: a neo-populist delight in rule-bashing that ignores the inevitable result of lawlessness, the end of due process for everyone. While the subversion of legal rules in *Mr. Smith Goes to Washington* has been denounced as "a horrible, hysterical reduction of the U.S. Senate to grotesque game show," *The Runaway Jury*'s cheerful endorsement of a caper that razes the American jury system is no less jarring.

At novel's end, Grisham's protagonists leave the law. They reject the messy contests of urban life to teach history, roam the world or stroll secluded beaches. *The Chamber*'s Adam Hall remains in practice after the resolution of his grandfather's case, but this is less an endorsement of law than a statement of faith in the New South.

Grisham suggests that the law as we know it will not permit his young idealists to achieve justice over the long term. This is true, of course. But it is his own view of law that stops his protagonists from effecting meaningful change.

GRISHAM'S AND CAPRA'S MIRACLE ENDING

Capra's stories have been criticized for resorting to "emergency exits," contrived finales where America's profound inconsistencies—democracy and capitalism, order and freedom, ethnic identity and community solidarity—are miraculously reconciled by love, or angels, or a well-timed heart attack.

Grisham resurrects the miracle ending with plots that depend on an astonishing juror (*A Time to Kill*), an extraordinary judge (*The Rainmaker*) or the unlikely genius of novices who trump every expert and elude every agency (*The Firm*).

These narrative escape hatches allow Grisham to avoid confrontation with the real evils that underlie his tales—not psychotic partners or obscure assassins, but the actual problems of contemporary American lives. Indeed, Grisham's books suggest that injury and injustice are dissolved in bright victories, the inevitable outcome of noble quests.

Yet Grisham's perspective sells law short. The recognition of our best and worst impulses, the reconciliation of a dozen disparate attitudes, the ticklish calculation of what we have finally saved or squandered is what law does best. In the end, his fictional worlds suffer not because they have too much law, but because they have too little.

TUROW'S GRIM VERITIES

If Grisham's novels tolerate no compromise, Scott Turow's bleak urban stories offer little else. In Turow's world, no answer is unambiguous, no truth untarnished, no conclusion uncorrupted. But Turow's fiction, like Grisham's, is also of a peculiarly American character. In grit and grimness, Turow's stories recall the dark pop-narrative style that emerged after V-J Day, film noir.

Set in unstable metropolitan environments, peopled by losers and loners, noir narratives—[movie director] Jacques Tourneur's *Out of the Past* (1947), [movie director] Orson Welles' *The Lady from Shanghai*, [movie director] Robert Siodmak's *Criss Cross* (1949)—captured the paranoia of the postwar period.

Honor and shame, guilt and forgiveness, devotion and deceit were classic noir themes. Turow's novels reimagine both noir's twisted characters and its tortured contrivances.

In *Presumed Innocent,* Turow's protagonist Rusty Sabich heads the search for a murder suspect who proves to be Sabich himself, a plot device from [movie director] John Farrow's *The Big Clock* (1948). [Main character] Sandy Stern's psychological autopsy of his dead wife in *The Burden of Proof* recalls [movie director] Otto Preminger's *Laura* (1944) and [movie director] Fritz Lang's *The Woman in the Window* (1945). *Pleading Guilty* (1993) proves to be exactly that, a sustained confessional in the style of [movie director] Billy Wilder's *Double Indemnity* (1944) and *Sunset Boulevard* (1950). Yet Turow's books invoke noir in atmosphere even more than in action.

Noir's complex stories looked like conventional tales of cops and killers, much as Turow's dense novels are labeled mysteries. Yet the noir film's labyrinthine streets stood in for the national subconscious, and its protagonist—the cynical postwar *Everyman* for whom [actor] Humphrey Bogart was the prototype—conducted less an investigation of crime than an inquisition into the American psyche. In the end, what the noir inquiry uncovered was the neurosis of the middle class in a seemingly placid era.

HEROES STYMIED BY THEIR OWN VALUES

For all their alienation, noir heroes were the embodiment of bourgeois certainties—bankers, detectives and insurance men who measured their lives by the actuarial tables. So, too, Turow's lawyers are emblems of the traditional verities, values as fixed as statute and as firmly grounded as common law.

Yet it is these very immutables that reach out to strangle Turow's conventional men. Turow's attorneys master law only to find that legal systems ensnare them; they seek love only to have it render them vulnerable; they forge human ties only to be borne down by obligations that even death cannot relieve.

Nor are the accepted truths of the hero's world any longer certain—corruption and decay are everywhere. The noir films commented on social disintegration with bold allusions to sexual perversity. So, too, Turow's scenes of outre [bizarre] sex are more political than prurient [lustful], his characters' seemingly endless physical humiliations standing in for wider inadequacies and despair.

THE HUMAN FRAILTY PORTRAYED IN TUROW'S STORIES

Human frailty lies at the heart of all Turow's legal narratives. His protagonists are themselves congenitally flawed, marked by alcoholism or illness or insecurity. These lawyers bring no unequivocal claims to justice, defend no pure clients.

Ultimately, they are hardly distinguishable from their antagonists, characters who are the protagonists' opponents in name alone—figures so deeply wounded, so capable of courage and cupidity, that they might in some other Turow novel be heroes.

A product of human endeavor, the law of Turow's world is eminently fallible. His cops cover up private transgressions; his judges hide public malfeasance. Corporate defendants profit from the death of hundreds; state prosecutors protect the culpable. Through myriad complexities of plot, Turow's innocents accept responsibility for sordid crimes; his guilty remain un-charged. Ineffectual in what we label its objectives, the law of Turow's world—like the law of our own—seems to fail. This, Turow suggests, is because we have not understood what law is meant to do.

WHAT THE LAW CANNOT DO

Law does not, and cannot, solve the problems of the human condition. Indeed, Turow's strongest theme may be that law is without jurisdiction in the regulation of our most consequential connections, our ties to family.

Law is, rather, a measure of our willingness to involve ourselves in the business of life; of our impulse to mitigate misfortune. Law cannot prevent our suffering, as [Turow's character] Sandy Stern argues in *Burden of Proof*, yet it does what it can, ensuring that "the seas engulf only those who have been selected for drowning."

Admittedly, Turow's perspective on law may be seen as a dark one. Nevertheless, the final message of film noir was one of redemption. Noir's bruised protagonists sinned, and were called to task, and then, at last, were given peace. This is ultimately Turow's legal justice.

His practitioners fail, and judge themselves, and suffer punishment, and then go on. In the end, it is a world of law that embodies our faith rather than our final judgments. A world where legal practice is a form of prayer. A bar of justice where both good and evil wear an eminently human face.

IMAGES OF JUSTICE THAT STRUCTURE PEOPLE'S LIVES

"These images have been shown to structure people's lives in a powerful way, perhaps more powerfully than a judicial opinion," says Martha Minow, a professor at Harvard Law School, of Grisham's and Turow's popular fictions.

For lawyers, these books speak to our notions of how law is supposed to work in our lives. We are confronted by two choices: Grisham sees law as a process that doesn't work absent some extraordinary intervention, while Turow sees law as a complex organism with its own internal logic.

We sense from these depictions what others expect of us. Of what we, in turn, expect of ourselves. To do otherwise— to dismiss these works as "just a movie" or "only a book" ignores how the world around us has confirmed their truths.

John Grisham's Heroes Have Moral Pluck

William H. Simon

The heroes in John Grisham's novels exhibit a combination of resourcefulness and disregard for the law in the service of basic but informal values. Because they do not conform to the official ethics adopted by institutions like the American bar, these characters have what might be called "moral pluck." Like Atticus Finch, the hero in *To Kill a Mockingbird,* they are willing to sacrifice the letter of the law for what they perceive to be the greater good. William H. Simon is a professor of law at Stanford University.

In a speech to a North Carolina bar association during the Clinton impeachment crisis, [special prosecutor] Kenneth Starr invoked Atticus Finch as an ethical role model. Many people scoffed at what they took to be an implied self-comparison. Starr's zeal in pursuing President Clinton did not seem comparable to Finch's courage in defending a falsely-accused black man in a racist town, and the justice of Starr's cause was less clear than that of Finch's.

Yet the most important difference between the ethics of Kenneth Starr and those of the hero of *To Kill a Mockingbird* remains to be noted. At the climax of Harper Lee's novel, the hermit Boo Radley emerges from seclusion and kills the villainous Bob Ewell. He does so in defense of Finch's children, whom Ewell was trying to kill. In the novel's final pages, a fascinating development occurs. Finch and Heck Tate, the sheriff, agree to lie to the town by saying that Ewell died accidentally by falling on his knife. There is no question that the killing was justifiable. Nonetheless, the sheriff convinces Finch that the local court system, which has just sent the patently innocent Tom Robinson to his death, cannot be trusted to vindicate Radley. So, the sheriff persuades Finch to go along with the accident story. In other words, the novel concludes with Atticus Finch engaging in what today could only be called obstruction of justice. Finch initially resists the sheriff's suggestion with arguments that would have done credit to a House Impeachment Manager. He says it would set a bad example for children. He says it would encourage further lawlessness. He says it would be dishonorable. But eventually he yields, and the novel does not leave any doubt that, in doing so, he does the right thing.

The sheriff exhorts Finch in this scene to a quality that I call Moral Pluck. It involves a combination of transgression and re-sourcefulness in the vindication of justice. Moral Pluck is per-vasive in favorable portrayals of lawyers in recent decades. . . .

In informal legal ethics discussions, a variety of rhetorical tropes are routinely deployed to penalize independent judg-ment. When lawyers appeal to informal norms of justice to explain either violations of enacted law or refusals to push client interests to the limits of enacted law, they are charged with self-righteousness and self-aggrandizement: "playing God," "arrogating power to herself," "imposing her own val-ues," "undermining the established process." In the academic literature, frequent disapproval of discretionary norms is linked to concerns about "accountability." Although it is not always clear to whom accountability is sought, it usually ap-pears that the authors contemplate control by the state.

The moral premises of popular fictional portrayals of lawyering are often quite different from this Conformist tradition. Popular fiction is anti-categorical and anti-authoritarian. Categorical norms require us to disregard all but a narrow range of the particularities of the situation. But fiction is committed to particularity. These works tend to evoke situations in which general norms are at war with more powerful particularistic intuitions. The authoritarianism of Conformist Moralism implies a consistently benign and reliable state. But popular culture warns that the state is often incompetent or corrupt and draws attention to the frightening and unjust consequences of its failings.

THE LEGAL POPULISM OF JOHN GRISHAM

John Grisham's novels exude a populist contempt for government and big business. They give us a creepily titillating view of a world dominated by vast criminal conspiracies. The conspiracies are identified with the mob, political terrorist organizations, or large corporations. They are operations of staggering power, integration, and efficiency. Agents of the government often play willing parts in them, but more often are simply too selfish, arrogant, or stupid to check them.

Grisham is also populist in seeing ordinary people—that is, people who are not mobsters, millionaires, or government bureaucrats—as more than occasionally good and capable of effective resistance to evil. Most of Grisham's books are coming-of-age novels that chronicle the moral growth of a new lawyer. The hero learns two lessons through participation in a series of adventures. First, you cannot plausibly understand legal or professional responsibility norms as the categorical injunctions they purport on their surface to be. To apply them in a manner that would make them worthy of respect requires a flexible, dialectical judgment. Second, to the extent the social order functions, it is not because of a system of promulgated rules more or less routinely enforced by a self-propelling governmental system of checks and balances, but through creative, transgressive moral entrepreneurialism on the part of individuals in crisis.

GRISHAM'S HEROES NEED TO BREAK THE RULES

These crises arise when the hero steps unwittingly into the midst of a conspiracy. It is a premise of thrillers of this genre that the hero would be foolish to respond to danger in the morally conventional manner. The morally conventional manner is to remain passive and law-abiding, and to rely on the government for protection from the lawless violence of the conspiracy. For the most part, however, the government is neither willing nor able to provide this protection. Its agents have been bought off, are pursuing selfish political agendas without regard to the interests of the people they are supposed to be protecting, or are simply reckless and stupid. Even where officials are more able and committed (and a few are), they are at a tremendous disadvantage vis-a-vis the menace. They have to play by the rules, while the mob and its analogues do not. The mob can shoot people in the back, torture, and bribe; the government generally cannot.

And, of course, the government, unlike the mob, can generally act only on the basis of proof. Grisham's novels are not detective stories organized around a quest by the hero to identify the villain. The hero and the reader know fairly early who the villain is. So do the police. The crisis arises from the fact that the government cannot act effectively in the absence of proof; a central impetus of the story is the hero's effort to get sufficient proof to enable or force the government to act.

In such situations, the hero has to extricate himself through cleverness and initiative. His efforts invariably require violations of various enacted norms. Sometimes the violations affront professional responsibility norms: Rudy Baylor in *The Rainmaker* engages in bedside solicitation of a personal injury victim. Gray Grantham, a reporter in *The Pelican Brief*, spies to discover the identity of a telephone source after promising not to do so. Sometimes the violations are major felonies: Baylor and Mitch McDeere of *The Firm* both commit homicides. McDeere's seems to be without legal justification or excuse, and although Baylor's might be legally excusable self-defense (or defense of another), he contrives an elaborate and flagrantly lawless cover-up.

Grisham clearly intends us to accept these actions as morally justified. When Baylor makes the bedside solicitation, he is on the verge of destitution (having been screwed by a prestigious corporate law firm that reneged on an agreement to employ him) and fully intends to do a good job for the client. Grantham plausibly believes that identifying the source may save innocent lives, including the source's. The two homicides are in self-defense and both victims are vicious predators (one a professional killer), but in neither case could the law, the police, or the courts be trusted to vindicate the hero.

In three early novels—*The Pelican Brief*, *The Chamber*, and *The Rainmaker*—Grisham delivers his moral lesson explicitly through dialogue. In *The Pelican Brief*, a law student, Darby Shaw, stumbles into a conspiracy that has led to the murder of two Supreme Court Justices. Chased by killers, she teams up with Gray Grantham, a *Washington Post* reporter, who is introduced as a "serious, ethical reporter with just a touch of sleaze." The detective on whom he occasionally calls for "dirty tricks" likes him because "he was honest about his sleaziness," not "pious" like his peers.

Grantham plays an important "trick" in the story. An anonymous source phones him repeatedly, indicating he knows something about the conspiracy but feels unable to work up the courage to pass it on. Grantham traces one of his calls to a pay phone and sends his detective to watch the phone. When the source phones next, Grantham signals the detective, who photographs the caller at the pay phone.

AN ETHICAL ISSUE CONCERNING NEWS SOURCES

When he shows Darby the picture at a time when killers are hot on their trail, she immediately raises the ethical issue:

"I take it he didn't just pose for this."

"Not exactly." Grantham was pacing.

"Then how'd you get it?"

"I cannot reveal my sources."

"You're scaring me, Grantham. This has a sleazy feel to it. Tell me it's not sleazy."

"It's just a little sleazy, okay? The kid was using the same pay phone, and that's a mistake."

"Yes, I know. That's a mistake."

"And I wanted to know what he looked like."

"Did you ask if you could take his photograph?"

"No."

"Then it's sleazy as hell."

"Okay. It's sleazy as hell. But I did it, and there it is, and it could be our link to Mattiece."

Grisham does not appear to intend irony or humor in portraying his characters as concerned with this matter of professional ethics at a time when their lives and indeed the fate of the republic are in jeopardy. Even Darby's statement that Grantham's ethical lapse is "scaring" her at a time when she has just survived two murder attempts is not supposed to be funny, just charming. But Grisham does judge Darby as naive. The photograph does no harm to the source, and does in fact turn out to be a critical link to the villain. The implication is that willingness to engage in a small, considered amount of "sleaze" is essential to being effectively "ethical."

An Ethical Issue Concerning Lying to Authorities

In *The Chamber*, a young lawyer and a law professor organize a group of students to make repeated phone calls to the governor, falsely identifying themselves as local voters, and urging him to grant clemency to a death row convict. As the hero explains to his sister what's going on, she asks:

"Is it legal?"

"It's not illegal."

"Is it ethical?"

"What are they planning to do with Sam?"

"Execute him."

"It's murder, Carmen. Legal murder. It's wrong, and I'm trying to stop it. It's a dirty business, and if I have to bend a few ethics, I don't care."

The sister's ethical qualm arises from the hero's deception

of a constituted authority, the governor. But the novel has made clear that the governor is cynically indifferent to the moral values of the clemency decision. The ethics the hero has to "bend" in order to avert "wrong" are the categorical precepts of Conformist Moralism.

FRAUD: CAN IT EVER BE A JUSTIFIED RESPONSE?

The Rainmaker also contains an elaborate telephone fraud, which the book portrays as a justified response to unlawful conduct, on the part of an opposing lawyer. However, the most explicit ethics discussion occurs earlier, when the hero is schooled by a sleazy but decent paralegal on the bedside solicitation of accident victims, a flagrant professional responsibility violation, but one that does no harm here and probably benefits the victim.

"You see, Rudy, [Deck says] in law school they don't teach you what you need to know. It's all books and theories. . . . It's an honorable calling, governed by pages of written ethics."

"What's wrong with ethics?"

"Oh, nothing, I guess. I mean, I believe a lawyer should fight for his client, refrain from stealing money, try not to lie, you know, the basics."

Rudy finds that a more succinct statement of the valid principles of legal ethics than anything he recalls from law school.

"But [Deck continues] what they don't teach you in law school can get you hurt."

Not only is solicitation the only way he can make a living, it is in the interest of at least the clients he solicits. They plan to do a good job for their clients, and if they refrained from soliciting, someone else would get them who might not be as loyal to them.

Again, the way to virtue involves transgression and resourcefulness. . . .

These entertainments usefully remind us that there is a moral orientation with broad popular appeal that is neither categorical and authoritarian on the one hand, nor relativistic on the other. They raise doubts about the view that has influenced both the Bar [American Bar Association] and the Congressional leadership that moral precepts framed in categorical and authoritarian terms are most likely to be compatible with ordinary moral thinking. For the appeal of these works seems to depend on a capacity for contextual judgment and a principled skepticism toward authority.

The second potential contribution of these works is substantive. They offer an ethical perspective that competes with Conformist Moralism as a source of moral guidance. The tone of this perspective is Emersonian. It is an ethic of self-assertion that encourages us to think of morality as an occasion for creativity. By contrast, the tone of Conformist Moralism is Puritanical and Kantian. It is an ethic of self-restraint that emphasizes the need to curb our more aggressive and destructive impulses through deference to external authority. Moral Pluck insists that ethics is not simply a matter of duties to society, but rather of character and personal integrity. While philosophers have argued for this perspective abstractly, popular culture teaches it by urging us to identify imaginatively with an attractive figure and then confronting us with the damage to the character's commitments and self-conception that deference to authority sometimes would require.

THE WIDESPREAD CORRUPTION OF OFFICIAL INSTITUTIONS

At the same time, these works insist that we take account of situations in which norms of authority are in tension with substantive justice. They remind us incessantly of the widespread ineptitude and corruption of official institutions. At one extreme—in the darker Grisham novels—these institutions are integral parts of a vast criminal conspiracy. . . . The works also remind us of the limitations of categorical norms that arise from their unresponsiveness to vital dimensions of some morally urgent situations. The confidentiality norm is the most prominent example. Many of these works try to demonstrate that the Bar's established norms are potentially incompatible with morally plausible responses to situations with high stakes. These are important lessons, and Conformist Moralism is deficient for ignoring them. Its view of the good lawyer is unattractive in its passivity and complacency.

Nevertheless, the type of popular works we are considering have undeniable limitations as a form of ethical reflection. One familiar complaint is that popular culture oversimplifies. Instead of promoting reflection, it gratifies unconscious desires for self-assertion by abstracting away the most important moral and strategic difficulties of real world ethical dilemmas. Some of us get visceral satisfaction watching Clint Eastwood or Sylvester Stallone blow away bad guys unconstrained by due process or physical limitations, but on reflection we do not regard their characters as role models. These fantasies grossly understate the dangers of transgressive self-assertion and underestimate the importance of institutional authority.

Grisham's Novels May Oversimplify the Ethical Dilemma

The works considered here are more self-conscious and thoughtful about ethics than the typical Hollywood "action" movie. Still, it has to be conceded that, as ethical discourse, they are unambitious. To begin with, the dilemmas they portray tend to take a Manichean [dualistic] form with implausible frequency. The works mislead by suggesting that, in the situations where lawyers perceive a tension between the dictates of established authority and their conceptions of substantive justice, defiance of authority would usually meet with the approval of most ordinary people (at least if they knew the facts). In fact, popular moral values are strongly divided across a broad range of situations. There are many situations in which many people would find unattractive the substantive values lawyers would assert in good faith defiance of constituted authority: Racists and fascists are rarely portrayed in the movies or on television as self-consciously principled, but no doubt some of them are. Moreover, if passivity and unreflective deference are unattractive, moralistic self-assertion can be so too. [Literary critic] Lionel Trilling's complaint—that the "liberal imagination" tends to ignore that "the moral passions are even more willful and imperious and impatient than the self-seeking passions"—is pertinent to the works discussed here.

The attitude expressed in these works toward institutions is also fanciful. The problem is not that they exaggerate the ineptitude and corruption of official institutions, though they probably do. More importantly, they portray Moral Pluck exclusively as an individual matter. The protagonists accomplish their heroic feats by themselves, or with the informal help of a few close friends. And their own transgressive initiatives leave no institutional traces. They do not contribute to new, more satisfactory institutions or alter the basic contours of established ones. . . .

In Grisham's novels, the hero's achievements rarely become public. The downfall of the villain is presented to the public as the work of established institutions, and the official ineptitude or corruption that required the hero's Moral Pluck is covered up. This trope reinforces the crude populist premise that we are surrounded by corrupt powers that determine our fate, but that we cannot see or influence. The hero redeems himself morally, helps some people, perhaps even averts a catastrophe, but he never changes the system. Thus, a deep pessimism about the larger society co-exists with a romantic view of individual initiative.

Is Moral Pluck Impractical?

This hostility to institutions is a further objection to Moral Pluck as an ethical ideal. For one thing, Moral Pluck seems implausible as a practical matter. As the solitary exploits of Clint Eastwood and Sylvester Stallone seem physically implausible, those of the prodigies of Moral Pluck seem to depend on unlikely assumptions about the capacity of even extraordinary individuals to manipulate people and institutions. On reflection these exploits do not inspire emulation: We plausibly doubt our ability to accomplish them by ourselves.

Moreover, the life of these heroes seems unattractively lonely . . . despite their amazing successes, Grisham heroes rarely achieve satisfying careers, especially as lawyers. They have a tendency to leave the profession. The heroes of *The Firm* and *The Partner* drop out of society entirely for lives of luxurious seclusion. Rudy Baylor of *The Rainmaker* gives up law to become a high school teacher. . . .

Moral Pluck—a combination of transgression and resourcefulness in the service of virtue—is a pervasive theme in some of the most prominent favorable portrayals of lawyering in recent popular culture. As ethical discourse, these works suffer from a preoccupation with extreme situations, a tendency to oversimplify the dangers and difficulties of independent ethical decisionmaking, and an unreflective suspicion of institutions. Nevertheless, as social data, the works are useful in indicating how different popular moral understanding may be from established professional norms. And in their insistence on the limitations of categorical norms and constituted authority, they are a valid corrective to biases of professional responsibility doctrine.

Grisham's Inconsistent Position on Portrayals of Graphic Violence

Joel Black

Joel Black writes about the legal battle between John Grisham and Oliver Stone. In 1996 Grisham wrote an essay blaming Stone's highly acclaimed movie *Natural Born Killers* for copycat murders committed by a teenage couple from Oklahoma. The couple watched the movie numerous times before randomly shooting two people in Mississippi, killing one and paralyzing the other. As a result of Grisham's essay, Patsy Byer, the paralyzed survivor of the shooting spree, filed a lawsuit against Stone and his distributors for a reported $20–30 million in damages. Joel Black examines the inconsistency of Grisham's condemnation of Stone's cinematic portrayals of violence and Grisham's portrayals of violence in his own work. If Stone is liable for damages because of cinematic portrayals of violence, then Grisham should be too. Joel Black is associate professor of comparative literature at the University of Georgia. He is the author of *The Aesthetics of Murder: A Study in Romantic Literature and Contemporary Culture* (1991).

What are we to make of John Grisham? Up until last year [1996], no one seemed more successful at integrating the roles of lawyer and novelist. Since 1991, at least one new best-selling novel appeared each year—*The Firm, The Pelican Brief, The Client, A Time to Kill*—that spawned yet another blockbuster movie focusing on some sensational aspect of the

Joel Black, "Grisham's Demons," *College Literature*, vol. 25, Winter 1998, p. 35. Copyright © 1998 by *College Literature*. Reproduced by permission.

judicial system. Then, apparently forgetting his own artistic affiliation with Hollywood, Grisham launched his own crusade against director Oliver Stone. What began in the spring of 1996 as a literary critique of Stone's 1995 film *Natural Born Killers* had escalated by June into an all-out, real-life legal battle.

GRISHAM BLAMES DIRECTOR OLIVER STONE IN COPYCAT CRIMES

Grisham's essay "Unnatural Killers" appeared in a southern literary journal he co-publishes, the *Oxford American*. The essay blamed Stone's film for the March 7, 1995, murder of a Mississippi cotton-gin manager named William Savage and for the shooting the following day of Patsy Byers in Ponchatoula, Louisiana, which left this part-time convenience store clerk paralyzed from the neck down. A teenage couple from Oklahoma was arrested for the crimes, and the girl, Sarah Edmondson, testified that she and her boyfriend, Benjamin Darras, had seen *Natural Born Killers* numerous times before driving off in the direction of Memphis with the vague notion of attending a Grateful Dead concert. Sarah reported that during the drive Ben couldn't stop thinking about Stone's film, and "spoke openly of killing people, randomly, just like Mickey spoke to Mallory" before those two fictional lovers in *Natural Born Killers* began the killing spree that resulted in more than fifty deaths. Diverted from their Memphis destination, Ben and Sarah wandered into Hernando, Mississippi, where Ben allegedly shot and robbed Savage in his office.

Then, wrote Grisham, just as "Mickey encouraged Mallory to kill," Ben urged Sarah to do the same. Grisham took Sarah's explanation for shooting Patsy Byers as further evidence of the influence of Stone's film (influence which Sarah herself has rejected): just as Mickey and Mallory were pursued by demons, Sarah "didn't see a thirty-five-year-old woman next to the cash register" when she pulled the trigger, but a "demon."

Clearly, Grisham was doing his own bit of demonizing. Alleging that the film was made "with the intent of glorifying random murder," he argued that Stone and the studio executives who produced the film were legally responsible for Ben and Sarah's crime. "A case can be made that there exists a direct causal link between the movie *Natural Born Killers* and the death of Bill Savage." Grisham then proceeded to propose a legal remedy that the families of victims might seek in cases of media-mediated violence—i.e., cases of murder at a distance or homicidal speech that actually entail an indirect "causal link" between media-statement and murderous act.

THE IMPLICATIONS OF MOVIES AS PRODUCTS

Think of a movie as a product, something created and brought to market, not too dissimilar from breast implants, Honda three-wheelers, and Ford Pintos. Though the law has yet to declare movies to be products, it is only one small step away. If something goes wrong with the product, whether by design or defect, and injury ensues, then its makers are held responsible.

In June 1996, an attempt was made to take the "one small step" recommended by Grisham: Patsy Byers brought a lawsuit against the "Hollywood defendants" (Stone and his distributor) for damages which the *LA Weekly* reported to be between $20 to $30 million. Even if the film is found to be only one of several contributing factors in the crime (and a small one at that), Stone and company will be liable under Louisiana law for 50 percent of the damages.

The case hinges on the legal and aesthetic issue of whether a commercial film should be considered as an instance of artistic expression protected by freedom of speech arguments, or whether it is a manufactured and potentially dangerous commodity covered by product liability laws. But while lawyers on both sides marshal their arguments, several related issues are worth noting:

The same special "crime" issue of the *Oxford American* in

which Grisham's editorial appeared also contained an essay entitled "Murder and Imagination" by novelist Donna Tarrt, who speculated about the possibility that Jack the Ripper had read *Dr. Jekyll and Mr. Hyde* and had used Stevenson's novel "as a kind of blueprint for his own unprecedented crimes." Noting that "the similarities are numerous and striking," Tarrt proceeded to make a case for what, if true, would be the most sensational instance of literature-mediated murder in history, far outstripping his precursor Jean-Baptiste Troppmann's 1869 slaughter of a family of eight after reading Eugene Sue's novel *The Wandering Jew*, Mark David Chapman's murder of John Lennon after poring over *The Catcher in the Rye*, or John Hinckley, Jr.'s attempted assassination of President Reagan after seeing the film *Taxi Driver*. It's just as well that Tarrt can't confirm her hunch; otherwise, following Grisham's argument, a case could be made—indeed, would have to be made—for taking legal action against the Stevenson estate and against the producers of all the cinematic adaptations of this tale.

GRAPHIC VIOLENCE IN GRISHAM'S WORK

Grisham himself is hardly immune from his attack on the producers of crime stories. Citing his novel *A Time to Kill*, in which a man "murders with clear premeditation two young racists who raped his 10-year-old daughter (a rape which Mr. Grisham writes about in horrifyingly graphic detail)," Stone facetiously argues that "according to Mr. Grisham's logic, the next time a 'righteous' revenge murder takes place (or, for that matter, the rape of a child) he will be happy to assume liability if it can be shown that the offender had read or seen *A Time to Kill*." In fact, one reader responded to Grisham's *Oxford American* essay by citing a recent cage in which a California woman killed a man who had molested her son. The respondent quipped that he expected Grisham to accept "responsibility for this killing, since it resembles the plot of his fine novel, *A Time to Kill*, and [to pay] a huge amount of money to the family of the child molester." Of course, this is unlikely because, as First Amendment lawyer Floyd Abrams has said, Grisham's "books, modest from a literary perspective, are not like breast implants. They are fully protected First Amendment speech, and the notion of judging them from some almost undefinable negligence standards is very troubling." In his campaign to condemn the artistic products of others on moral and legal grounds while assuming the innocence and integrity of his own work, Grisham loses much of his credibility. "The fact is," Stone observes, "Mr. Grisham has become a very rich man off a body of work which utilizes violent crime as a foundation for mass entertainment."

Playing the Media Card in Trials

In his editorial, Grisham predicted that an eventual "large verdict against the likes of Oliver Stone, and his production company, and perhaps the studio itself . . . will come from the heartland, far away from Southern California, in some small courtroom with no cameras." Originating in Tangipahoa Parish, Louisiana, Byers's suit indeed seems to fulfill this real-life script. Evidently Grisham expects such a rural venue to deter the presence of cameras in the courtroom, and to prevent Stone and his cohorts from playing the media card like that other controversial Hollywood defendant, O.J. Simpson, in his criminal trial. But this line of reasoning is hopelessly entangled in contradictions and in Grisham's own conflict of interest. Apparently it's O.K. if his own dramatic courtroom-centered novels are staged before Hollywood's cameras, but it's forbidden to broadcast real-life courtroom proceedings in which Hollywood filmmakers stand trial for their allegedly irresponsible camerawork.

Over the past five years, the key legal issue involving the news media has shifted from their failed legal battle to broadcast "live" executions of prisoners to their ongoing case-by-case struggle to broadcast sensational courtroom trials a la *Court TV*—a struggle that has become far more challenging in the aftermath of the O.J. Simpson and the Menendez brothers trials. Now that the news media have lost the right to film actual executions and are facing the prospect of having their cameras banned from sensational trials, the entertainment media stand to enjoy exclusive rights to present compelling courtroom and death-row dramas—albeit of a fictional or simulated nature—to eager audiences. That's just fine with Grisham, as long as competing Hollywood products that deal primarily with fictional scenes of murder like *Natural Born Killers* are kept off the screen.

THE DIFFERENCE BETWEEN GRISHAM'S AND STONE'S PORTRAYALS OF VIOLENCE

Of course, as Stone points out, murder scenes are by no means absent from Grisham's novels or their cinematic adaptations. The key difference between Grisham's portrayals of murder and Stone's in *Natural Born Killers* is that the former are placed in (and subordinated to) a judicial context, a narrative about the Law in which the killers are invariably exposed and brought to justice by the System. No such moral resolution is depicted in Stone's film, and I suspect that this is what really gets Grisham's goat. What he finds intolerable about *Natural Born Killers* is not Mickey and Mallory's mindless violence, but their escape from prison. As he describes the film's ending, "they free themselves, have children, and are last seen happily rambling down the highway in a Winnebago."

THE PROBLEM WITH GRISHAM'S PERSPECTIVE

An obvious problem with Grisham's aesthetic and legal perspective is that it is informed by a rigidly conservative ideology. He falls into the same trap that troubled Bob Dole during his 1996 presidential campaign when he selectively blamed Stone and other Hollywood filmmakers for fomenting social violence, but was careful not to include the *Terminator* films, starring Republican stalwart Arnold Schwarzenegger, in his indictment. Grisham's double-standard is still more blatant in that he sees fit to assail Stone's film without assessing the impact on viewers of the hugely popular movies based on his own novels. Moreover, as film critic David Denby has noted, the roots of this hypocrisy lie even deeper:

> There's something pathetic about Bob Dole's calling for restraint from Time Warner, when it's precisely the unrestrained nature of capitalism that conservatives have always celebrated. Conservatives would make a lot more sense on the subject of popular culture if they admitted that the unregulated marketplace, in its abundant energy, is amoral, that it inspires envy and greediness, that it shreds "values" and offers little space for encouragement for what William Bennett calls "virtues."

WHY GRISHAM'S POSITION IS OPEN TO ATTACK

Grisham's analogous call for commercial filmmakers to exercise artistic restraint, while he reaps windfall benefits from the unregulated marketplace, is open to attack. The spirit of corporate capitalism no longer tends to support, but all too often flagrantly contradicts, the Protestant ethic promoted by leaders of the religious right.

Indeed, the moralizing ethic that informs Grisham's argument is more troubling than its conservative ideology. According to this ethic, displays of physical violence and abuses of justice are acceptable as long as the Law reestablishes and re-asserts itself at the end. In contrast to these conservative fictions of the Law, Stone was drawn in the case of *Natural Born Killers* to a script that subversively revealed the irrelevance, if not the fictionality, of the Law in a media-saturated culture. Such a vision of the Law-as-fiction was bound to outrage a lawyer-turned-writer like Grisham. Similarly, Stone's earlier film *JFK* infuriated journalists and historians for suggesting that official "historical" accounts of events like President Kennedy's assassination were largely fabricated; if that were so, then Stone was entitled to offer his own scenario of the event, mixing fact and fiction, as he was later to do with the personal life and political career of another president in the film *Nixon*. One wonders: if Grisham's legal argument was to be accepted, and *Natural Born Killers* was found to have directly or indirectly caused William Savage's death and Patsy Byers's paralysis, could similar suits then be brought against *JFK* and *Nixon* for character assassination, alleging these films to be products that irreparably distorted the reputations of public figures, falsified the historical record, and warped the minds of young, impressionable viewers?

Grisham thinks he has found a way with his movies-qua-product argument to get around Denby's assertion that "there is no way in law of curtailing exploiters without also curtailing artists." While the law determines whether, in cases like that of Patsy Byers, Hollywood movies are to be considered primarily as instances of artistic expression, or as commercial products like cigarettes that are potentially legally liable for harmful effects on consumers, the question remains whether the law itself has a conflict of interest when it tries to adjudicate films like *Natural Born Killers* in which the Law doesn't prevail in the end.

CHAPTER 3

Themes and Issues in Grisham's Novels

Idealism Versus Institutional Corruption

G. Thomas Goodnight

G. Thomas Goodnight suggests that the popularity of Grisham's story, *The Firm*, is rooted in Americans' deep skepticism about the viability of social institutions. Goodnight shows how Grisham portrays his main character, Mitch McDeere, as being betrayed by law enforcement and the legal profession, both institutions he should be able to trust. Grisham places his protagonist in the position of having to be completely self-reliant. Popular fiction like *The Firm*, Goodnight says, appeals to a generation that is already predisposed to be suspicious of their elders. Goodnight is professor of communication studies at Northwestern University.

The novel *The Firm* is one of a series of works by Grisham (himself a law school product who was "thrilled" to escape the profession) that exploits suspicion of the law and animosity toward lawyers. Formally, the text translated into film is a cross between two novels-turned-films of another generation. Like *All the President's Men, Firm* is a story that traces how young professionals bring down a corrupt public institution while finding personal success; yet, Grisham's and Pollack's narratives extirpate questions of justice and focuses exclusively on whether any tactics of personal and professional survival will work. Like I. Levin's *The Stepford Wives, Firm* debunks small-town virtues by exploring the high costs of conformity. In the 1990s, the victims are no longer housewives in suburban chains, but a young, dual-income couple whose

G. Thomas Goodnight, "The Firm, the Park, and the University: Fear and Trembling on the Postmodern Trail," *The Quarterly Journal of Speech*, vol. 81, August 1995, pp. 267–90. Copyright © 1995 by *The Quarterly Journal of Speech*. Reproduced by permission.

family commitment is sorely tested by the demands of institutional reason. Thus, Grisham and Pollack jettison the political messages of an earlier generation while sustaining a style that offers "a cynical vision of the human condition and a disdain for all institutions." What remains is a deftly told tale that amounts to an extended chase scene, interrupted only by bits of expositional discussion, formed loosely as a mystery.

A young attorney is lured from Boston to the wilds of Memphis by a silk-stocking firm. Enacting the vision of Yuppie Utopia, the law school graduate, Mitch McDeere, and his spouse, Abby, get a new designer home, new BMW 318i (Mercedes-Benz 300 Cabriolet in the film), and a new set of friends who seem at first a warm, glamorous, idealized "family." Abby becomes a little suspicious when an associate's wife tells her that having children is "encouraged by the firm," but working-wives are all right, too. "How do they do that?" she asks. But, the prospects of successful employment overwhelm these small worries as the couple looks forward to the challenges of upscale living.

THE FIRM'S POSTMODERN THEMES

Firm, both novel and movie, inverts the American dream with a profusion of postmodern themes that appear to well up from a Baudrillardian fun house. The fun begins in the stately uptown offices of Bendini, Lambert & Locke whose marble-lined, neoclassical spaces and rows of well-manicured library shelves are but (what else?) gleaming facades that divert attention from the shadowy, labyrinthine machinations of power. We see the work of the firm as a faux reality, where the mettle of new attorneys is tested by assignment of fake cases, and where young associates are subjected to surveillance systems. Psychological hiring profiles assure that all recruits will meet these challenges and become pillars of the community; but, just in case, the firm induces its members to follow a traditional code of propriety—a wife and children, not for community values but to ensure that associates can be controlled once implicated in the firm's work.

A TRAP OR AN OPPORTUNITY

The McDeeres, of course, are unaware of all of this at first. Mitch thinks that work is an opportunity for personal achievement in an *agôn* to be first among elite litigators. Suspicions arise, however, when he and Avery Toller, Mitch's mentor in the ways of legal practice, meet with a tough-minded tax-account client on the Grand Caymans. They all agree that what they are up to is a "game" that has "nothing to do with the law," but when Avery tells the entrepreneur that he is being a bit tough on young Mitch, Sonny Capps responds vaguely that at least he doesn't break legs and stuff like the people in Chicago. Is this just a manner of speaking or is there something to it? Suspicion is fed further by the "accidental" deaths of two associates, an unlikely event that is brought to notice by a "chance" encounter with two seedy FBI agents. In fact, all those who have tried to leave the firm meet with death purportedly by accident, they tell him, a material improbability that generates curiosity for Mitch, leading first to incredulity, then suspicion, and eventually to the unraveling of all the young couple's institutional loyalties. But this is not a simple tale of a single corrupt institution.

Skepticism is fed continually in novel and film alike by Mitch McDeere's intermittent contacts with government agents, who, like the partners of the firm, play the young attorney and his family as a pawn in clandestine games of institutional power. The "terror" brought on by successive, secret narratives of complicity and punishment, elaborated to McDeere by warring representatives of the law, motivates his need to invest faith in a dwindling circle of intimates and to escape institutional battles. Yet, the spreading realization of duplicity within and across institutional communication retards such action because each strategic choice results in the discovery of further threats.

ESCAPING INSTITUTIONAL BATTLES

There is no escape because McDeere is cornered by a particularly vicious simulation of the prisoner's dilemma: if he turns in the firm, then he violates client confidentiality and loses his legal career; if he remains silent, then he will be prosecuted when the firm takes the fall. Furthermore, McDeere's brother Ray is in prison: if McDeere doesn't accede to the FBI, there is little chance of parole. If he betrays the firm, there are ways of reaching Ray, too. Finally, as a last resort, he confides in his wife about all (in the movie) or most (in the novel) of these machinations, including the fact that their house is bugged. Recognizing that even their most intimate communications have been the target of surveillance, Abby panics and runs blindly down the street. Later, she comes to see that the only solution is to join Mitch and to play a double game. Before going back inside their home to stage conversation for hidden tape recorders, Abby finds a postmodern moment. Quietly, she murmurs, "Somewhere, inside, in the dark, the firm is listening."

Could it be that, in this world of remaindered justice, all personal relationships are manipulated to serve a corrupt system and that nothing is beyond the global reach of modernist institutions? Mitch has the answer to this rhetorical question. Once he discovers the real game, he sheds all his modernist values but keeps wearing the Armani suits (one of the firm's tokens of power). While he maintains the appearance of participating in normal discourse, he acts at a distance, doubling the code, using it, and finally absorbing the power of the firm. He and Abby gradually gather evidence of illegal acts, all the while distancing themselves from discovery. Moreover, in the novel the means of conquest are appropriate to a postmodern world, for the success of the McDeeres comes from mastering electronic fund transfers, while the vulnerability of the firm is lodged in its old fashioned preservation of text based records, which is turned from asset to liability by photocopying the "real" evidence of money laundering. Rather than run through the repetitive episodes of duplicity and institutional manipulation that merely unfold more of the same, let us pause and explore the aesthetic resources deployed for constructing what has been called "the last class-action hero."

BECOMING MORE EFFICIENT THAN THE FIRM

The novelist Grisham and the film director Pollack concur on one thing: McDeere is brilliant, sensitive, indeed outstanding even at Harvard—traditional accoutrements of modernist heroes. Yet, within the aesthetic spaces plumbed here, no brilliant dialogues are to be found; there are simply no compelling legal arguments, philosophical insights, or dialectical engagements, nor can one find even an especially cunning psychological strategy. Most of the dialogue resembles bar room talk, but remember that it is will, not reason, that confirms genius in the postmodern moment. As J.F. Lyotard avers, in postmodernity even basic "competence" founded on the ability to distinguish true from false, just from unjust, "no longer makes the grade." And so the lawyer is more than competent, he is brilliant, because once he discovers that the stakes of the game are nothing but power he becomes tactically driven, engaging in dangerous play that scrupulously requires that each institutional standard be regarded as mere convention, and every contract, legal and otherwise, as free-floating signifiers—all in the interests of becoming even more "efficient" than the firm. Thus, the young attorney moves from imitating his seniors, who ostensively gain social standing through the public trials of legal practice, to donning for himself the ritual mask of power.

Postmodern heroism is a flee[t]ing role, however, for it runs its course within an unstable aesthetic gap between identification with intimates and mimicry of elites. Thus, in the novel McDeere races a solipsistic marathon strategically negotiating his way around good and evil in a breakneck ride on the shifting appearances of loyalty and subversion in an escape to—

nowhere. Ultimately, in the novel Mitch McDeere ends up trying to elude nearly everyone—government agents, the mob, associates and partners, his mother, the concierge at a cheap hotel on the Gulf Coast—while cleaving to his wife and brother, with the only solace being $8 million he "scammed" from the mob and the FBI, a criminal act that author Grisham passes over forgivingly. After all, it's really not the young attorney's fault that everyone else is so corrupt. So at novel's end, the small McDeere family slips quietly beyond the ken of institutional power altogether—nervously setting sail with no particular island paradise in mind. They take only a moment to ponder the meaning of it all.

> "Are you scared, Mitch?" [asks Abby at last]
>
> "Terrified." [he responds]
>
> "Me too. This is crazy."
>
> "But we made it, Abby. We're alive. We're safe. We're together."
>
> "But what about tomorrow? And the next day?"
>
> "I don't know, Abby. Things could be worse, you know. . . . There are worse things than sailing around the Caribbean with eight million bucks in the bank."

THE FIRM'S FILM ADAPTATION

The film *The Firm* is a "faithful" Hollywood adaptation, by which I mean that it absorbs the publicity of the book and turns around its mood by producing an ending with a difference. Through exploiting the believable, if trivial, social knowledge assumption that lawyers over-bill, actor Tom Cruise (playing Mitch McDeere) is able to pull off a counter-scam by gathering evidence of mail fraud in falsification of time sheets for firm customers, including the mob! (One might wonder why sophisticated, successful and rich attorneys would permit themselves to become vulnerable for such comparatively trivial and dangerously acquired sums, but coherence and plausibility do not seem fit criteria for this art.) The evidence brings down McDeere's partners, bargains off the government, and enables the young professionals to return back to Boston, poor but with their ideals, lawyerly oath and marriage intact, together with the blessing of the Chicago mob, which—in a comic turn—agrees to have Cruise represent them against their former law firm.

Some critics felt that the new movie-ending was "priggish" because of its storybook purity, but this is no 1930s melodrama or comedy. Rather, the film's ending indulges the audience in a schizophrenic moment, for while McDeere remains an idealist (family man and professional to the core), his brother Ray, the soulful ex-felon, and Tammy, a trace romantic element of the old hard-boiled detective novel genre, in the end set sail on the Caribbean without Mitch and Abby, but with all the purloined government money and "good cooking" they can handle. Cynically, Hollywood induces its audience to affiliate with status quo ideals while enjoying an escap(ad)e on the margins, all for the price of a $6.50 ticket, a $19.95 video cassette, or a $3.00 rental.

A GENERATION X INTERPRETATION

Try as I might, I cannot resist speculating on what these "works" look like to the "me-generation," which rode the Reagan recovery to Wall Street excess, only to crash in the stock market collapse and banking scandals and to merge via MTV with its younger peers as members of Generation X— a chaotically ordered ensemble whose chief historical entry point into the social world was seeing their own economic prospects diminished as well as their forty or fiftysomething mentors fired in a decade of corporate downsizing, takeovers, and flight. For all this ripe-to-be-disillusioned audience, the mass media dramatize the lessons (or pander to collective suspicion, depending on one's anchor of reflection) that not only are elders morally fatuous, worse than corrupt they are strategically inept. Moreover, fellows of the twenty or thirtysomething generation who buy into institutional life, not rejecting socialization out of hand as sheer hypocrisy, appear as even greater fools, non-players really. Their lot, at best, is to join the "legions of sniveling Boomer yes-men . . . gathering cobwebs in middle management, preventing *you* from getting anywhere." Only the postmodern hero makes out and moves on, either in the novel as strategic tyro or in the film as idealist-cum-sensualist (have it your way). The seamless web of privatized suspicion and fleeing the code, in fragmented forms, pervade both media thereby giving a whole new twist to the term "escapist fiction."

Grisham's Version of an Age-Old Formula

Martha Duffy

Although he has been pummeled by his reviewers, Grisham's background as the son of an itinerant construction worker and as a lawyer helps him succeed with an age-old formula: the little guy triumphing over the big guy. In the case of *The Rainmaker*, the novel's protagonist, Rudy Baylor, is the scrambling young law-school graduate who is battling a giant insurance company that turned down claims that might have saved the life of a young man dying of leukemia. Trying to learn from critical reviews of his past work, Grisham includes more character development and humor in *The Rainmaker*. Martha Duffy finds that the effort has paid off. The novel made its debut at number one on the best-seller list in a first printing of 2.8 million copies. Duffy writes for *Time* magazine.

John Grisham has shown a rare gift for creating suspense. But there's no suspense anymore about what happens when a new Grisham novel hits the bookstores. His latest [in 1995], *The Rainmaker*, has just made its debut at No. 1 on the best-seller list; its first printing of 2.8 million copies set an all-time record. When Hollywood offered a mere $6 million for the movie rights, the author temporarily withdrew his book from the market. After all, he got the same amount for his last movie sale, *A Time to Kill* and the only direction Grisham can see is up. Each of his first three best sellers doubled the sales of the previous one. Total sales of his six novels to date: 55 million copies. Worldwide box-office take for the three movies (*The Firm, The*

Martha Duffy, "Grisham's Law," *Time*, vol. 145, Fall 1998, p. 87. Copyright © 1998 by Time, Inc. Reproduced by permission.

Pelican Brief, The Client) made from his books: $572 million.

Writing even a single best seller is one of the few ways a person can generate riches solely by his own efforts, and Grisham is enjoying it to the fullest. At 40, he has little patience for the rites of celebrity. He gives few interviews and signs books mostly at stores that helped him out when he was driving copies of his first book around the South. He has even moved away, temporarily, from the dream house he built on a 70-acre spread in Oxford, Mississippi, because too many tourists were coming down from Memphis after buying a tour package that included Elvis' Graceland and Grisham's farm. He now hides away in an exclusive country preserve near Charlottesville, Virginia.

PUMMELED BY REVIEWERS

It's a wonderful life, almost too good to be true. Grisham is rich and handsome (the only novelist on *PEOPLE* magazine's list of the 50 most beautiful people this year), with a happy family (a wife and two kids), a religious faith (Southern Baptist) and the vast and varied world of entertainment at his feet. Too good, it seems, not to attract some criticism. Like most widely popular novelists, he has been pummeled by reviewers—for paper characters, bad dialogue (not true; he writes realistic talk), disappointing endings. Ray Sawhill, in *Modern Review,* says Grisham's books "aren't Middle America as seen and expressed by an artist; they're Middle America entertaining itself. A Grisham novel is cousin to those catalogs you find in the seat pockets of airplanes."

There are rumbles too from the author's former Shangri-La. A rancid attack by Atlanta-based free-lancer Ed Hinton in January's *GQ* charged that Grisham is sullying the sacred ground where Faulkner once trod: "In a long line of Mississippi writers, Grisham is a singular aberration and paradox, the worst and the richest, the least distinguished and the most popular." The article outraged most locals, who point out that Grisham helped pay to repair the Faulkner estate and rescued a new literary periodical, the *Oxford American*. Says novelist Barry Hannah, who has a formidable reputation but not Grisham's millions: "I guess in America if a guy gets some fame and celebrity, he can't seem to do anything right."

Grisham's fame and fortune are based on the law. The son of an itinerant construction worker, he graduated from the University of Mississippi law school and practiced criminal law for nine years in Southaven, outside Memphis. The experience gave him his particular take on an age-old formula: little guy triumphs over big guy. Or over the feds, the Klan, the Mafia, the CIA, the FBI—or, in *The Rainmaker*, the insurance industry.

AN AGE-OLD FORMULA: LITTLE GUY TRIUMPHS OVER BIG GUY

Rudy Baylor, the novel's protagonist, has just graduated from law school and is scrambling for legal work when he happens upon an excellent case: a giant insurance company has repeatedly turned down a claim for a procedure that might have saved the life of a young man dying of leukemia. His efforts get Baylor caught up in every kind of deadly trap that Big Business and big law firms can lay.

Grisham has said he reads reasonable reviews and tries to learn from them, and *The Rainmaker* shows evidence of that. Though the plotting is crafty enough, it lacks the dervish pace of such earlier novels as *The Firm* and concentrates more on character and even humor. Baylor and his "partner," a fellow who has flunked the bar for 15 years and calls himself a paralawyer, are really ambulance chasers, and their desperate lunges after a subsistence income are a little like *Roadrunner* sketches. Baylor, for example, studies for his own bar exam in the cafeteria of a local hospital, the better to zero in on the newly maimed. As a page turner, the book is very smart—until a resolution that, like *The Firm*'s, is a bust. Bowing to bestseller formula, Grisham introduces a love interest for Baylor, but she is of little use except to get the author out of his plot.

It may be that Grisham simply disapproves of smut—or else he can't write sex scenes and knows it.

GRISHAM IN HOLLYWOOD

No matter; Hollywood can fix that. Screen rights to *The Rainmaker* will probably go for $7 million to $8 million. Initial bids were less than expected, according to reports, because a ponderous 750-page draft of the novel was leaked prematurely (editing later streamlined it to 434 pages). But how can Hollywood resist another No. 1 best seller from a writer who, like Michael Crichton and Tom Clancy, is as bankable as the biggest movie stars? Says screenwriter Akiva Goldsman, who adapted *The Client* and will do *A Time to Kill*, based on Grisham's first novel: "He shoots you into the story and then takes his time letting it play out. He's a formidable engine." Early in his career, Grisham was indifferent to Hollywood, but its allure seems to be growing on him. He has script approval on *A Time to Kill* and is a consultant for a new CBS series based on *The Client*. He is also writing an original screenplay about a lawyer in the toils of a seductress.

Still, he keeps in touch with the folks back home. Last week he returned to Blytheville, Arkansas, not far from his birthplace of Jonesboro, for a book-signing jamboree. The crowd was big and enthusiastic; they regard this gracious Southerner as an old acquaintance. The feeling is mutual. Grisham goes back because Mary Gay Shipley, the owner of That Bookstore in Blytheville, was an early booster. He may be Hollywood's hottest author, but Grisham remembers his friends.

Grisham's Impossibly Noble Protagonists

James Bowman

James Bowman observes how Grisham's hero in *The Street Lawyer* reflects the tendency in Washington, D.C., and in the country as a whole, to adopt an outward image of concern without the corresponding ideological commitment. Bowman refers to these people as stylish figures striking cool attitudes. *The Street Lawyer* features a protagonist who leaves his six-figure income to work for a legal clinic, betraying his wife's and his family's expectations for his future. To Bowman, the character seems caught up in his own image, congratulating himself for breaking free of his bourgeois past and doing good deeds. Bowman denounces Grisham for writing novels about impossibly noble characters who leave their careers to work for the poor, while he, Grisham, becomes wealthy off of the stories of these self-sacrificing souls. James Bowman is American editor of the *Times Literary Supplement*.

The Washington novel used to be about politics and power, sex and scandal, elections and intrigue among capital insiders. If John Grisham's latest is anything to go by, the new Washington novel will be, as Washington itself increasingly is, about image. Since the invention of the music video, people seem to have stopped expecting popular entertainment to provide much in the way of plot or characterization or serious themes or, indeed, anything but a succession of stylish figures striking cool attitudes; and Grisham has brought the ethos of the music video to popular fiction. Not

James Bowman, "Lawyer-Chic," *National Review*, vol. 50, April 6, 1998, p. 51.

that Grisham himself should be blamed for this state of mind. It is everywhere in Bill Clinton's Washington. Even Phyllis C. Richman, the restaurant reviewer for the *Washington Post* writes of a trendy local eatery: "Look around the dining room . . . and you'll guess you are seeing academics in D.C. for a conference, journalists not with sources but with gossip pals, lawyers who wouldn't work for corporations but only for public-interest groups."

Clearly, the hint that working for "public-interest groups" is a fashion statement is not something that originated with John Grisham. But Grisham—who, if he chose to, could count his novels toward his own pro bono resume, since they amount to unpaid public-relations work for the Trial Lawyers Association—is making the most of this new lawyer-chic. His latest hero, Michael Brock, a 32-year-old associate in anti-trust law with one of the biggest and most prestigious Washington firms, is briefly taken hostage by a homeless street person who calls himself "Mister." After managing to slip past security, Mister terrorizes a number of lawyers at Michael's firm with a firearm and what he pretends is dynamite strapped to his body; he is eventually shot and killed by a police SWAT team.

GRISHAM'S HERO QUITS HIS CUSHY JOB

Michael was standing behind Mister when the bullet hit and, though unharmed, continues to be haunted by his captor's challenges to his fellow K Street fat cats. What has he done for the poor and the homeless? How can he continue to take home his six-figure salary and look forward to millions more after he makes partner, he muses, when the Gingrichite hordes are throwing more and more people into the streets every day? So he quits his cushy job and joins a store-front "street law" clinic supported by a charitable foundation and run by a big-hearted, street-smart black lawyer called Mordecai Green. Michael's new salary is only $30,000, with few benefits. But there is hope of better things to come. For on his way out, he stole a file from his old firm which implicates the fat cats in illegal activity that led to the deaths of a single mother and her four children. He and Mordecai happily set about suing his former colleagues for millions.

He also divorces his wife, who is not prepared to take the cut in pay (but whom he is tired of in any case), and he worries his bourgeois parents and greedy corporate-lawyer brother. He is very proud of himself. "I even looked the part," reflects the preening Michael as he sits in his new office; "My beard was more than a week old; my hair was slightly over the ears and showing the first signs of unkemptness; my khakis were wrinkled; my navy blazer was rumpled; my tie was loosened just so. The Nikes were still stylish but well-worn. A pair of horn-rimmed glasses, and I would have been the perfect public-interest lawyer." Michael is the kind of guy who is always catching little glimpses, like that one, of himself in the mirror of his own inspiring story, and this novel which tells his story often reads like a tour through somebody's scrapbook. "There I am helping a junkie kick her habit, feeding a homeless person, marching in a demonstration against uncaring government," he tells us proudly—and he (or Grisham) expects us to coo our approval.

PREENING OVER HIS OWN GOOD DEEDS

Here, for example, Michael again watches himself as he sits in his new office: "If my dear brother Warner could've seen me sitting there on Sunday, shivering at my sad little desk, staring at the cracks in the plaster, locked in so that my potential clients couldn't mug me, he would've hurled insults so rich and colorful that I would've been compelled to write them down. I couldn't comprehend my parents' reaction . . ." But we know he really loves it. "Look at me!" he all but cries in narcissistic glee. "Aren't I the very devil for defying my boring parents and brother and their selfish, middle-class, workaholic values?" He is even a little bit in awe of himself and the splendor of his sacrifice. As he contemplates going to work for

Mordecai and the poor people, he tells us, "My soul kept me awake most of the night. Did I have the guts to walk away? Was I seriously considering taking a job which paid so little? I was literally saying good-bye to millions. The things and possessions I longed for would become fading memories."

Many's the tear that will doubtless roll down, glistening, from beneath the frames of designer sunglasses on beaches across America when those words are read. Yet neither Grisham nor his hero ever demonstrates the slightest shame at making the poor street people, none of whom is given any depth of character or individuality to speak of, mere props in the drama of this yuppie paragon. His creator obviously shares young Michael's high opinion of himself and believes, as Michael believes, that the street lawyer cuts quite a figure in his blazer and beard and fashionably well-worn Nikes. And he does, too. But it is not the figure of a hero of the mean streets so much as it is that of a conscience-stricken yuppie like his creator.

GRISHAM: A BRAND NAME AMONG NOVELISTS

Small wonder that Grisham has made himself into a virtual brand name among novelists—the DKNY Dickens or the Starbucks Stevenson. Instead of leaving his own riches and working for the poor, he writes novels about impossibly noble characters who leave their riches and work for the poor—and so he makes more money! It's the perfect set-up for him, painlessly quieting his own qualms while he dominates the best-seller lists by exploiting the huge market of well-paid, college-educated professionals who read four books a year and would have everything if they could find a clear conscience for themselves at The Sharper Image. He tells them that everything is OK so long as they hold the right political opinions (the Republicans are repeatedly traduced here) and contribute something to the public-interest lawyers who live off the welfare state and occasionally get to make life miserable for the fat cats.

Moreover, Grisham has given his less fortunate legal brethren a dream of escape from the tedium and the nastiness and the work and the corruption of the legal profession. It is a dream not of life in wrinkled khaki trousers and Nike tennis shoes as a public-interest lawyer like that poor mug, Michael; it is a dream of life as a rich novelist like himself. Now every third lawyer and law student in the land has a partly completed novel or screenplay in his bottom drawer. And who can blame these young lawyers? They are under no illusions that their professional lives will be devoted to the righting of wrongs and the pursuit of justice; they know that their hopes of wealth from lawyering are tainted. Far better, then, to get rich by thinking up stories about imaginary lawyers—selfless and idealistic lawyers who do well by doing good. Not to mention that it is a lot easier work and you don't have to commute.

Grisham Departs from His Usual Story Line

Malcolm Jones with Ray Sawhill and Corie Brown

In his review of John Grisham's novel *The Testament*, Malcolm Jones discusses how Grisham departs from his usual story line of the small idealist protagonist battling a powerful and corrupt institutional giant. In this novel, Grisham's tenth, the protagonist is a forty-eight-year-old attorney, Nate O'Reilly, with a substance-abuse problem. Nate is sent to the Brazilian back country to track down a missionary/heiress, a journey that turns into a spiritual quest. In an interview with the author, Jones asks Grisham if Nate O'Reilly's concerns are Grisham's own concerns. Grisham talks about his struggle with wealth but denies autobiographical connections with his protagonists. Malcolm Jones writes for *Newsweek*.

It doesn't take much to make John Grisham happy. He relishes a good cigar. He adores baseball in general and Little League in particular. But maybe more than anything, the 44-year-old author loves his privacy, because he knows all too well what it's like not to have any. Currently Grisham and his wife and two children live on 204 very private acres outside Charlottesville, Va. That's as much as he wants anyone to know because four years ago the Grishams were living more or less under siege in Oxford, Miss., prisoners of his overnight success. After the publication of his second novel, *The Firm*, in 1991, Grisham the lawyer and state legislator became Grisham the celebrity author. "People suddenly felt the need to come visit us," he recalls dryly. "Complete strangers who had a manuscript or an idea for a book or a movie would just come to the house and knock on the door, ready to drink coffee."

So what he's saying, then, is that the life of a celebrity can be pretty rough, right?

Grisham grins. "Hey, I'm a famous writer in a country where nobody reads."

It's a nice line, you want to tell him, but it says more about his self-effacing manner than it does about his actual status as the best-selling author of the decade, with 110 million books in print. On Feb. 2, [1999], the day it was published, Grisham's latest novel, *The Testament*, outstripped the first-day sales for his previous novel by 40 percent at Barnes & Noble and 62 percent at Sam's Club, according to Double-day. The new novel had a first printing of 2.8 million, and the publisher went back for a second printing in the first week. His success—along with Scott Turow's—has helped make the legal thriller one of the most popular genres. Movies have been made from six of his 10 novels, and four, including *The Firm* and *The Client*, were huge hits.

As part of an elite handful of mega-selling authors that includes Stephen King, Danielle Steel, Michael Crichton and Tom Clancy, Grisham has literally taken bookselling to places it's never been before—not just to airport kiosks but to price clubs and, most recently, online bookselling. Grisham's thrillers have also given publishing a global spin. American best sellers are now worldwide best sellers. Grisham has been translated into 34 languages, and he's been a No. 1 best seller in eight countries, even ones where the legal system is entirely unlike the American model he writes about. And uniquely among that elite club of mega-selling authors, his audience cannot be corralled into a discernible demographic. He sells to everyone, from teens to senior citizens, from lawyers in Biloxi to housewives in Hong Kong.

The big criticism that dogs the appearance of every new Grisham novel is that he's writing the same book over and over (David and Goliath go to court). Not this time. Abandoning the courtroom for the Brazilian jungle, *The Testament* proves that Grisham can spin an adventure yarn every bit as well as he can craft a legal thriller. Yes, once again the hero is a lawyer. And the villains are slimeballs. Make that unregenerate slimeballs. And the good people, particularly the missionary heroine, might as well wear wings and halos. But Grisham plays the legal stuff, if not for laughs, then certainly for its satirical value. The main event is the spiritual resurrection of Nate O'Reilly, a 48-year-old hotshot lawyer with two busted marriages, a big problem with drugs and alcohol, and a way of treating rehab like a hobby.

The Testament begins with the suicide of billionaire Troy Phelan, a mean, eccentric old coot who cuts his legitimate heirs out of his will and leaves his $11 billion to his illegitimate daughter, Rachel Lane, a missionary in Brazil. The story doesn't get into gear, though, until Nate's firm dispatches him to the Brazilian back country to track down the heiress. Before he can find her he endures a tropical storm and a plane crash. Following that up is a boat ride chartered by Joseph Conrad and navigated by Edgar Rice Burroughs, and we haven't even gotten to the jungle fever and rubbing knees with the missionary lady.

Maintaining Popularity

Like all Grisham's books, *The Testament* is a compulsory page turner with a subterranean pull as old and potent as myth. "His books grab you on a deep emotional level," says director Joel Schumacher, who's made two films from Grisham's books, including the superb *The Client*. Ironically, although Schumacher says that "Grisham's books are movies," Hollywood hasn't had a chance to make one since *The Rainmaker* in 1997. Grisham has refused to sell the film rights to his last three novels, because, he says, the marketplace was just getting too crowded with Grisham stories (he's had as many as three paperback titles chasing each other up and down the best-seller list simultaneously). "You just can't imagine how many ways things can go wrong with turning one of these stories into a movie," he says.

The best analysis of a Grisham plot comes from a screenwriter—Oscar winner Robert Towne. Scriptwriter on the movie of *The Firm*, he recalls his dismay when he first began untangling Grisham's tortured plot. "You remember the Danny Kaye monologue in *The Court Jester* about the 'pellet with the poison's in the vessel with the pestle, but the chalice from the palace has the brew that is true.' That was *The Firm*. I thought, this is going to be tough." But the more closely he examined *The Firm*, the more he admired it. "It's a wonderful paranoid fantasy," he says. "All the horrible things you can imagine happening to you do happen."

A SPIRITUAL QUEST?

It's the same with *The Testament*, only this time the paranoia and the horrible things are vanquished when the physical journey turns into a spiritual quest for Nate midway through the novel. Grisham himself is a lifelong Baptist. As a boy, "whenever we moved, the first things we did were join the church and get our library cards." Things haven't changed much. Both Grisham and his wife have been Sunday-school teachers, and he has made numerous trips to Brazil with church groups to build houses and clinics. He contemplated a full-blown Christian conversion scene for Nate. His wife and his editor talked him out of it. What readers get instead is an intriguing and never pious story of a man's search for spirituality—as a sort of bonus, Grisham tosses in a nasty critique of materialism. "Success had brought him nothing but misery," he writes of Nate. "Success had thrown him in the gutter." A strange novel, yes, but ultimately quite moving. And since quality of life and the quest for faith are hot-button issues for baby boomers these days, the story of baby boomer Nate's rejection of the material world should resonate with readers.

And what about Grisham? Are Nate's concerns his concerns? "We have struggled at times with wealth," Grisham says slowly. "We've been very lucky and very fortunate. The point I was trying to make with Nate was that if you spend your life pursuing money and power, you're going to have a pretty sad life. But no, there's none of me in Nate." At this point, his wife, Renee, speaks up. "When you're successful all of a sudden, the way we were, there is a lot of guilt." Looking over at her husband, she says, "I think in John's books that he does try to resolve that subconsciously." Grisham is staring off into space, and it's easy to see that as far as he's concerned things are getting a . . . little . . . too . . . personal. Suddenly he says, "Let's take a walk. Do you smoke cigars? Let's fire up a cigar and go for a walk."

Better yet, let him show you his Little League ball fields. No sooner had he arrived in Charlottesville than he decided the town's ball fields were inadequate and inaccessible to rural kids. So he financed the construction of Cove Creek Park—six baseball diamonds, batting cages, clubhouse—a Little League heaven on earth that tells all you need to know about Grisham's generosity and his determination.

GRISHAM'S EARLY SUCCESS

"John is a handshaking, friendly, open person," says his friend Richard Howorth, who runs Square Books in Oxford. "But there's depth there." Grisham is the average guy who married the girl next door, but he's also the boy who gets up every morning at 5 to write. Ten years ago, he strode into Howorth's bookstore to say he'd written a novel and he'd appreciate it if Howorth would hold a book-signing party for him. And, by the way, he needed to sell 500 copies. Howorth told him he'd be lucky to sell 50 (he sold 49), but he took *A Time to Kill* and promised to read it. "And sure enough, like everybody, I was up until 2 in the morning." *A Time to Kill* sold about 5,000 copies. Republished after *The Firm* appeared, it sold 292,000 hardback copies. A copy of that very first edition, signed by the author, will fetch $2,500.

According to Howorth, "none of the literary people in Oxford carry a grudge about Grisham's success," because he is so genuinely unassuming about his own writing. "I don't pretend it's literature. It's high-quality, professional entertainment," Grisham declares. Not surprisingly, he compares his career to an athlete's arc. "You have some really good years where you're on top, and then one day it's over. I won't always write a book a year. I won't always write about lawyers. Once the legal thrillers run their course, I'd like to get back to telling stories about the South and Ford County [the fictional setting of *A Time to Kill*]." Does that mean that this collector of Faulkner first editions thinks of himself as part of the great Southern literary tradition? "Oh, no. I could have grown up in Denver and written *The Firm*," he says. He pauses to take a long pull on his cigar. "I think one day I'd like to become a Southern writer." Another pause, another puff. "Yeah, that's my goal, to become a true Southern writer." He allows himself a small grin. "Who also sells a few copies. In my lifetime."

A Grisham Novel with No Lawyers

Jeff Zaleski

Jeff Zaleski interviews John Grisham about why he departed from the genre of legal thriller in *A Painted House.* Grisham denies writing the novel to change how the critical establishment views his work. Instead, Grisham says the impetus for writing *A Painted House* came from a desire to try something new. The novel, first published serially in the literary magazine the *Oxford American,* is based on old family stories as well as experiences from Grisham's own childhood. Grisham plans to return to writing legal thrillers. Jeff Zaleski writes on John Grisham and other authors for the trade magazine *Publishers Weekly.*

Jeff Zaleski: A Painted House *has no lawyers. What happened to the lawyers?*

John Grisham: Oh, they'll be back. This is a very momentary departure from the legal books.

Why did you write this novel?

It's an accumulation of old family stories, most of which are probably fiction anyway, that I've heard all my life. At some point a few years ago, the big stories came together, so I included a lot of family history and scrambled it together with a big dose of fiction and came up with what I thought was a good story. And I think after you write a number of books in a certain genre, you have the urge to try to something different.

Do you have any hopes that this novel might change how the critical establishment looks at your work?

Jeff Zaleski, "*Publishers Weekly* Asks John Grisham: What Happened to the Lawyers?" *Publishers Weekly,* vol. 148, January 22, 2002, p. 178. Copyright © 2002 by *Publishers Weekly.* Reproduced by permission.

No, I gave up on those folks a long time ago. I think I've sold too many books to ever be taken seriously by those folks. But it certainly has not hurt anything. I'd be horrified now if I wrote a book the critics loved. My career'd probably be on the downslide.

Then you may be in trouble now.

[Laughter] The problem with literary criticism is that the critics are other writers. And they can be very mean. Can you imagine Bruce Springsteen reviewing Bob Seger's CD? And if you don't write "literature," whatever that is, then you're pretty much condemned. But I think the people who read popular fiction don't read a whole lot of reviews, or if they do, they pretty much ignore them.

So how will people who read popular fiction respond to this book?

I really don't know. I think they're going to like it because there's a real story there. It's not the stay-up-all-night-call-in-late-for-work kind of Grisham book, but the pages do move along. You got some diehards out there who thrive on the legal stuff by me and Turow and Baldacci and Steve Martini [best-selling authors of legal thrillers], and I don't know how they're going to react.

There are some minor differences between the serialized novel and the published book, most notably that the epilogue has been lopped off.

Yeah, well, we cut that out. I wasn't sure about it when we published it. I liked it at the time, Marc [Smirnoff, editor of the *Oxford American*] really liked it; David [Gernert, Grisham's editor and agent] didn't, Steve [Rubin, Doubleday publisher] didn't, my wife didn't. It was kicked around at length. At the last minute, I said, "Let's not do it."

You say the book is inspired by your own childhood. Did you actually pick cotton as a kid?

Oh yes, for the first seven years of my life. The setting is very accurate. That house and that farm and that town are very, very similar to my grandparents' house and farm and the town of Black Oak, where I spent the first seven years of my life.

You really succeeded in getting into the head of a seven-year-old for your narrator.

I'll tell you, the biggest challenge was to keep him as a seven-year-old. I think at times the kid's a lot smarter than any seven-year-old would be. I kept stretching it, I kept asking myself how much would a kid know and remember and see.

This is the sort of novel that, without your name on the cover, probably would be considered midlist and get a much smaller printing. Someone said to me, "You know, Grisham can put his name on a roll of paper towels and get it printed in two million copies. And for the amount of money he probably got for this, they could have fostered dozens of books by midlist novelists." What do you think of that?

Well, you could say that about every book I write, or Clancy or King or Crichton or every one of us who gets a lot of money for our books. The truth is, and Stephen King made this comment years ago, if we turned the money down, they wouldn't use it to foster 20 novels, they'd use it to go after another big novel. But I don't hear stuff like that, so it doesn't bother me. I'm not in the publishing world. I'm on a farm in Virginia.

Let's wait and see if people enjoy the book. If it falls flat, then I got overpaid. If it sells a lot of copies, well, I'm trying to write high-quality popular fiction. Don't criticize me for writing popular fiction when a lot of people enjoy it. This may be different. If people are disappointed, and it's not going to sell like the other books, then, yup, I should have put my name on a roll of toilet paper, I guess.

This book is different. Are you doing anything different to promote it?

Not a thing. I'm going to New York on February the 5th, and I'll be on the *Today Show* February the 6th, and do a couple of interviews. I'm going to sign at a bookstore here in Charlottesville, as always, and do the same for bookstores around Memphis, as I've done for 10 years. And then it's time for baseball season.

I'm curious about what you think of e-books, when you don't even use e-mail much.

Very rarely. I work on a computer in my office, in a separate little building here on the farm, and there are no telephones there, and the computer is not online. But I've given some serious thought to trying something online. Something different. Not a short story and not a novel, but something in between. One mistake I think a lot of authors make is, they make it to the top and the books tend to get thicker, ponderous. They become bricks. I'm going in the other direction. I'm thinking about trying a story that's maybe 100 pages long. Something you could sell online and let people download and print it and read it.

Will you do that through Doubleday?

I don't know. We haven't gotten that far, I haven't got the thing written yet.

Grisham's Hero Faces a New Kind of Dilemma

David Corn

In his review of John Grisham's most recent novel, *The Summons*, David Corn of *Nation* magazine discusses how Grisham breaks away from his usual formula of modern-day David versus Goliath. Instead of fighting institutionalized corruption, his hero in *The Summons* must deal with unexpectedly finding $3 million in cash among his deceased father's personal effects. Although the effect of the discovery on the protagonist is the story's main concern, Grisham does create a subplot of corporate greed versus the individual: His hero discovers corporate corruption in a pharmaceutical company. This leads Corn to conclude that Grisham's stories do stimulate social concern; according to Corn they are "Not quite a *Nation* editorial, but better than Sydney Sheldon."

A few years ago I concocted a theory about John Grisham I was too lazy to prove. Here was the hypothesis: This best-selling author was the most successful popularizer of populist notions in American culture. His stories—on paper and on-screen—often pit small folks against malicious corporations and their anything-for-a-buck lawyers who manipulate a system that favors monied elites. In *The Pelican Brief* a rapacious oil developer looking to drill in the environmentally precious marshlands of Louisiana funnels millions to government officials and bumps off two Supreme Court Justices to thwart a lawsuit brought by public-interest lawyers against his wildlife-threatening scheme. In *The Rainmaker*, a young lawyer bat-

David Corn, "Populism: The Thriller," *Nation*, vol. 274, April 8, 2002, p. 31.

tles a mega-firm on behalf of a couple screwed over by an insurance company that won't cover a bone-marrow transplant for their son, who is dying of leukemia. *The Runaway Jury's* bad guy is Big Tobacco. In *The Street Lawyer*, a corporate attorney bolts from his firm when he discovers it's been wrongfully evicting poor people from their homes. Justice for sale. Money in politics. Corporate greed and malfeasance. And millions of readers devour this stuff.

But not me. I was interested in this notion of Grisham the Populist, based on reading the book reviews and seeing several Grisham flicks. After tearing through *The Pelican Brief*—too breezy, too melodramatic, too unrealistic, even for airport fiction—I was not eager to do the heavy lifting necessary to confirm the theory (that is, read the books). Instead, I tasked an assistant to peruse some Grisham novels and draft plot summaries. In the meantime, I wrote Grisham and requested an interview to discuss the politics of Grishamland. Should face time be granted, I figured, I would crack open paperbacks in preparation. In the meantime, the summaries started appearing on my desk, and my assistant complained, "This is like reading television." But no word came back from Oxford, Mississippi. I deep-sixed Project Grisham.

Then recently the phone rang. A book review editor asked, "Didn't you once have some ideas about John Grisham?" "Well, uh, kind of, but I didn't really pursue it. . . ." Yet that was enough for this editor: The new Grisham was being FedExed to my office. I was back on the case.

GRISHAM DEPARTS FROM HIS POPULIST FORMULA

I was under no illusion that Grisham was a modern-day Steinbeck or Odets. He's not writing to send a message. And he does take his swipes at progressive-minded characters. The NAACP lawyer in *A Time to Kill* is an egotistical cad who cares more about money and power than helping a black man on trial for killing the two white men who raped his daughter. The anti-tobacco activists of *The Runaway Jury* use underhanded means to defeat the tobacco-industry lawyers. But by placing legal Davids in battle against corporate Goliaths to derive drama, Grisham has consistently presented an unflattering picture of the Enron class. However, his latest, *The Summons*, only marginally hews to such a story line. The main clash is not between the powerful and the screwed. It occurs within a family. There is an evil-corporations subplot, but it's mostly device, not driving force.

The setup: Ray Atlee, a 43-year-old law professor at the University of Virginia, receives a letter from his dying father, "The Judge," calling Atlee back home to Clanton, Mississippi, to discuss his father's estate. Atlee, estranged from Dad and the ancestral home, does not look forward to the trip. He's already in a funk. His ex-wife has married a millionaire corporate raider and borne him twins (conceived, all too obviously, while she was married to Atlee), and a lovely (and rich) third-year law student is teasing Atlee silly. So off he goes in his midlife-crisis sports coupe to the town he escaped. When Atlee arrives home, he finds Dad dead. Atlee dutifully starts organizing his father's papers and stumbles across a surprise: more than $3 million in cash hidden in twenty-seven stationer's boxes. Where did this poorly paid public servant get the moolah? What should Atlee do with all those Ben Franklins? Include them in the estate—which would mean the government would grab its share, his father's honor might be tainted and Atlee's alcoholic/junkie brother, Forrest, would claim half and be able to finance his descent into complete self-destruction?

This is a what-would-you-do mystery, and a how-would-you-do-it thriller. (We learn that three mil in hundreds fills three large garbage bags—and that poses logistical difficulties if you're driving a car with a small trunk.) Grisham throws in enough moral shading to supply Atlee reason beyond avarice to take the money and run. But greed hovers, even as Atlee tells himself he's not sure he's going to keep the loot. First, he has to uncover the backstory.

A warning to any potential readers of *The Summons*: There are a few plot points in this book, and to describe it further is to reveal precious twists. If you have an inclination to read this novel, do not continue beyond this paragraph. Skip ahead to the review of the Italian Baroque lady painter who specialized in blood-drenched scenes.

THE SUMMONS—AN UNSATISFYING TALE

OK, now that the Grisham fans are gone, let me say that this book is much better than the improbability-ridden *Pelican Brief*, but it was still unsatisfying. The main dilemma is engaging—what to do with free, albeit probably tainted, money?—yet there's not much oomph to the tale. Perhaps that's because Grisham does not provide reason for readers to care about Atlee. He's a good-enough sort, plays well with fellow faculty members, has been hurt by a woman who done him wrong and won't sleep with a student until she graduates. He specializes in antitrust, but we're spared his views. He's not the Jimmy Stewart type, drawn helplessly into an alternative world of intrigue. He's a guy who likes flying and is coasting. Until he finds the cash.

Atlee then faces three immediate challenges: how to move the money without being spotted, how to determine whether it's marked and how to discover its origins. Of course, he's able to succeed on each front, but the trouble is that these tasks end up not requiring great ingenuity. Also, there's someone trailing him, and that unknown person wants the cash and is willing to use violence to get it. Atlee has to watch his back as he shuttles to various rental-storage lockers (where he keeps the money) and to various casinos (where he drops hundred-dollar bills, looking to see if the expert money-handlers will detect them as marked). As for the money's source, Atlee's investigation is too straightforward. In the judge's papers, the files concerning one case are missing. Atlee heads to the Gulf Coast to examine the court records. He then talks to the lawyer who won. And—bing!—that mystery is solved, a bit too easily.

A HINT OF POPULISM

It is this case that brings us the novel's hint of populism. Seems a Swiss pharmaceutical behemoth was selling an anti-cholesterol drug that had an unfortunate side effect: kidney failure. The company was aware of the problem but marketed the drug anyway. By the time Judge Atlee came to be presiding over a wrongful death suit, filed against the company by a widow living in rural Mississippi, tens of thousands of kidneys had been ruined. The judge showed the company's lawyers no quarter and in the end socked the pharma with an $11.1 million fine. "The opinion," Grisham writes, "was a scathing indictment of corporate recklessness and greed. . . . [The] trial was Judge Atlee at his finest." How did this lead to boxes full of cash? I'll leave that to your imagination. Here Grisham is in sync with his past us-versus-them plots. But *The Summons* does not dwell upon the malfeasance of the drug-maker. Rather, the book blasts away at the attorney who won the case, in what amounts to an indictment of mass-tort lawyers. The pages drip with scorn for attorneys who become wealthy by handling class-action suits against corporate malefactors, such as tobacco companies and asbestos manufacturers. "I worship money," this lawyer tells Atlee. Grisham takes the bogeymen of the Naderish left and the Chamber of Commerce right—corporate evildoers and trial attorneys—and places them in a state of moral equivalence.

But this is far from the point of the book; it's simply the point of my review, for there's not much to dig into in *The Summons*. The solutions to the few mysteries in it are not big shockers. The novel contains just enough elegant touches to make readers realize there should be more. Atlee's difficult relationship with his brother is rendered well. The impact of the found money on Atlee is interesting to watch. Yes, watch—this is like reading television. . . . Atlee's desire to hold on to the bucks ends up threatening his comfortable life, and Grisham throws in a much-yearned-for curveball toward the end. For a moment, it looks as if Atlee might actually be facing time in the slammer. But fate is not that unkind. And who is it that's after Atlee? A reader who looks at this book as an English parlor mystery, wherein the culprit has to be someone in the room, will not be hard pressed to conjure up the answer.

Back to the important matter: my take on Grisham. He's certainly not writing leftwing agitprop disguised as legal-drama pulp. But in his universe, lustful and reckless corporations often run wild until they are checked by a righteous judge or some other soul moved by ideals, not dollars. Trial attorneys might be scumbuckets who care more about champagne baths than about their clients. Still, Grisham has the novel's annoying millionaire ambulance-chaser tell Atlee, "It takes people like me to keep 'em honest"—a proposition that neither author nor protagonist rebuts. *The Summons* does not advance the unsteady justice-ain't-equal populism of Grisham's previous work. That's not its mission. But in general Grisham presents the tens of millions who glide through his popcorn novels with the view—in some books more than others—that life is often unfair for a reason, unfair by design, and that specific interests are responsible for this. Not quite a *Nation* editorial, but better than Sidney Sheldon.

FOR FURTHER RESEARCH

Works by John Grisham

A Time to Kill. New York: Wynwood, 1989.

The Firm. New York: Doubleday, 1991.

The Pelican Brief. New York: Doubleday, 1992.

The Client. New York: Doubleday, 1993.

The Chamber. New York: Doubleday, 1994.

The Rainmaker. New York: Doubleday, 1995.

The Runaway Jury. New York: Doubleday, 1996.

The Partner. New York: Doubleday, 1997.

The Street Lawyer. New York: Doubleday, 1998.

The Testament. New York: Doubleday, 1999.

The Brethren. New York: Doubleday, 2000.

A Painted House. New York: Doubleday, 2000.

Skipping Christmas. New York: Doubleday, 2001.

The Summons. New York: Doubleday, 2002.

The King of Torts. New York: Doubleday, 2003.

About John Grisham

Martin Arnold, "Now, Grisham by E-mail," *New York Times*, January 29, 1998.

Ed Brown, "Grisham's High Ground," *Fortune*, March 16, 1998.

Current Biography, "John Grisham," September 1993.

Jennifer Ferranti, "Grisham's Law," *Saturday Evening Post*, March/April 1997.

Terry Gross, "An Interview with John Grisham," *All Things Considered*, National Public Radio, May 23, 1997.

Jeff Zaleski, "The Grisham Business," *Publishers Weekly*, January 19, 1998.

Reviews and Criticism

James Bowman, "Lawyer-Chic," *National Review*, April 6, 1998.

Cramer R. Cauthen and Donald G. Alpin III, "The Gift Refused: The Southern Lawyer in *To Kill a Mockingbird, The Client*, and *Cape Fear*," *Studies in Popular Culture*, October 1996.

CheckerBee Publishing, *John Grisham: A Reader's Checklist and Reference Guide.* Middletown, CT: CheckerBee Publishing, 1999.

Adrienne Drell, "Murder, They Write," *ABA Journal*, June 1994.

E. Ripley Forbes, review of *The Runaway Jury, Public Health Reports*, November/December 1996.

Steve Forbes, review of *The Partner, Forbes*, May 19, 1997.

Deborah Ford-Kaus, review of *The Client, Florida Bar Journal*, July/August 1993.

Michael Galen, review of *The Firm, BusinessWeek*, April 29, 1991.

David Gates, review of *The Runaway Jury, Newsweek*, May 27, 1996.

Malcolm Gladwell, review of *The Runaway Jury, New Republic*, November 4, 1996.

G. Thomas Goodnight, "The Firm, the Park, and the University: Fear and Trembling on the Postmodern Trail," *Quarterly Journal of Speech*, August 1995.

Michiko Kakutani, review of *The Street Lawyer, New York Times*, February 10, 1998.

David Keymer, review of *A Time to Kill, Library Journal*, June 15, 1989.

Verlyn Klinkenborg, review of *The Firm, New Republic*, March 14, 1994.

Peter S. Prescott, review of *The Firm, Newsweek*, February 25, 1991.

Aric Press, review of *The Pelican Brief, Newsweek*, March 16, 1992.

Frank J. Prial, review of *The Pelican Brief, New York Times Book Review*, March 15, 1992.

Mary Beth Pringle, *John Grisham: A Critical Companion*. Westport, CT: Greenwood, 1997.

Alexandra Rockey, review of *The Chamber, Insight on the News*, July 11, 1994.

Adam Sandler, "Grisham vs. Stone: 'Killer' Opponents— Murder Sparks Novelist to Call for Action," *Variety*, June 17, 1996.

John Skow, review of *The Chamber, Time*, June 20, 1994.

——, review of *The Pelican Brief, Time*, March 9, 1992.

——, review of *The Runaway Jury, Time*, May 27, 1996.

Pete Slover, review of *The Firm, ABA Journal*, April 1991.

Marilyn Stasio, review of *The Client, New York Times Book Review*, March 7, 1993.

——, review of *The Firm, New York Times Book Review*, March 24, 1991.

——, review of *The Street Lawyer, New York Times Book Review*, March 22, 1998.

Carl Sessions Stepp, review of *The Pelican Brief, Washington Journalism Review*, July/August 1992.

Films Based on the Novels of John Grisham

The Firm. Director Sydney Pollack. Paramount Pictures, 1993.

The Pelican Brief. Director Alan J. Pakula. Warner Brothers, 1993.

The Client. Director Joel Schumacher. Warner Brothers, 1994.

The Chamber. Director James Foley. Universal Pictures, 1996.

A Time to Kill. Director Joel Schumacher. Warner Brothers, 1996.

The Rainmaker. Director Francis Ford Coppola. Constellation Films, 1997.

INDEX